AGEING IN NORTH EAST INDIA
Tripura Perspective

AGEING
IN
NORTH EAST INDIA
Tripura Perspective

Edited By
Chandrika Basu Majumder
&
Paramita Saha

AKANSHA PUBLISHING HOUSE
NEW DELHI-110002 (INDIA)

AKANSHA PUBLISHING HOUSE
4649-B/21, Ansari Road
Darya Ganj, New Delhi - 110 002
Ph.: 23263193/9811582579
Fax: 011-23263193
Email: ektabooks@yahoo.com

Ageing in North-East India: Tripura Perspective

First Published 2008
ISBN 978-81-8370-145-7

PRINTED IN INDIA

Published by M.P. Misra for Akansha Publishing House, New Delhi and Printed at Aryan Enterprises, Delhi.

Contents

Section III
Social Security: Issues and Initiatives

Foreword

In the recent years, much literature on North-East India has been published by the scholars of this region on various issues related to the people and the region as a whole. However, the issues related to ageing, the elderly persons of this region are not properly addressed so far. Although every 1st October is being observed as the international day for the elderly, yet the magnitude of the problems of the elderly persons in North-East India is not properly addressed neither in the myriad seminars organized by various academic bodies and the NGO's nor their problems and aspirations are documented.

Considering the lacunae in this field, the Indian Council of Social Science Research, North Eastern Regional Centre (ICSSR-NERC), Shillong took the initiative to bridge the gap by organizing a series of State level seminars on the magnitude of the problems of the elderly persons in North-East during 2006-2007. This book has its origin in one of the seminars organized by the Department of Political Science, Tripura University, Agartala, Tripura during December 2006. Dr Chandrika Basu Majumder and her colleagues in the department took the keen interest in the seminar not only in organizing it but also compiling and revising the papers presented in the seminar in the present book format.

The papers carefully put together for this volume by Dr Basu Majumder raise some of the vital questions related to the elderly persons in the State of Tripura and will, I am sure, prove to be essential reading for anyone interested in the field of ageing.

ICSSR-NERC
Shillong

C. J. Thomas
Acting Director

Preface

Growing concern about the problems of the elderly population, in recent times stems from the realization that, prolongation of life span has become a reality for a large number of individuals all over the world leading to ageing of world population. The desire not only to live longer but also to live better, has motivated research on ageing issues.

Till the First World Assembly on Ageing that took place at Vienna in 1982 under the aegis of United Nations, literature on ageing was based almost entirely on the experience of the developed countries. Though the Vienna assembly posed the growing number of elderly in population as a global problem for the developing countries passing through the early phases of demographic transition the main concern was to identify the factors responsible for high fertility. The question of old age security finds its earliest mention in this context as an important motive behind fertility. The official document presented by the Government of India in Vienna projected the view that in India the elderly persons are well integrated with the society and there is hardly any problem of the aged. However much has changed since then and there have been various attempts to study the socio-economic context, the elderly person encounters in the later stage of life and the problems faced by them. The increase in the population of the elderly and the prediction that by 2016, the population of the aged could be doubled has made the government consider ways and means for adopting a positive action. The United Nations International Year of the Older Persons in 1999 drew attention to the marginalisation of the elderly persons in the development process and emphasized the need to develop 'a society for all ages'. This requires formulation of social security and health care policies keeping in view the needs of the elderly. The Second World Assembly on Ageing (Madrid, 2002) emphasizes the importance of incorporating the interests of older persons into national level policies and planning.

Impact of longevity and population ageing is pervasively affecting economy, family life, work patterns, health care, living arrangements, socioeconomic attitude, educational systems and many more. It is necessary to prepare individuals to adapt and build a positive attitude to an ageing society. As individuals are living longer, they should also have the opportunity to work longer and the working environment need to be congenial to the older workers. To stay active and productive in later life requires efforts both at the individual and social levels. A society must find ways to enable the elderly persons to continue to contribute to the family and society.

Ageing is a natural and irreversible process of human life. It is not a disease, nor a disintegrative force. But, the reference to the aged is often made in terms of social problem, as a burden or in need of adjustment. This kind of stereotyping of the elderly persons need to be replaced with a more realistic assessment of their contribution to the society.

According to the Census 2001, the total number of persons in the age group of 60 years and more is 2,32,549 in Tripura. In this context the need for research to generate information regarding specificities of local conditions becomes important, as the process and extent of integration of the aged to the society is culture specific. It is with this intention of generating state level information on Tripura that the seminar on 'Magnitude of the Problems of Elderly Persons of Tripura was organized by Department of Political Science, Tripura University in December, 2006 with financial assistance from ICSSR- NERC. The seminar brought together academicians, scholars and social activists working in this field. The book is primarily based on papers presented in the seminar covering different aspects of the ageing problem. These are arranged in three sections. Section I include papers on the demographic, socio-economic and cultural aspects of ageing. In the papers included in Section II the health issues of the elderly population of Tripura are examined. Social Security matters for the aged are considered in the papers in Section III.

In the paper on The Added Years of Life – Elderly Women in Tripura, Paramita Saha explores the ageing process of Tripura's population with special reference to the elderly women of Tripura and highlights the problems and needs of the increasing number and proportion of elderly women. The gender dimensions of the elderly population are captured on the basis of secondary data from census and primary data collected from field survey. It is observed that the magnitude and nature of the problems of elderly women is more acute compared to elderly men. They are economically and socially more vulnerable, a greater proportion of them being poor, alone, lacking assets and suffering from multiple diseases.

In his paper on 'Problem of Loneliness among the Elderly Persons of Tripura' Prof. Satyadeo Poddar observes that despite the historical-cultural tradition of care and respect for the elderly persons along with Governmental and Non-Governmental initiatives, the problems of loneliness of the elderly persons remain to be the least addressed. Loneliness is an emotional state in which a person experiences a powerful feeling of emptiness and isolation. A Study conducted by the Centre for Cognitive and Social Neuroscience at University of Chicago in 2006 found loneliness can add 30 points to the blood pressure reading for adults over the age of 50 years. The issue of loneliness among the elderly is studied in respect of residents of Mahatma Gandhi Old Age Home of State Infirmary, Government of Tripura, Narsingarh, Agartala. The author finds that the inmates of State Infirmary of Tripura do not feel lonely and depressed being away from home. They are quite satisfied with their life in the old age home and some even felt happier here than at home. They are not socially isolated; neither do they feel desolate. This becomes possible as they remain connected to their family outside the home. Though it is not possible to generalise that elderly residents do not experience loneliness in all old age homes in Tripura, the paper highlights the importance of close connection between the institution and home, the approach of the caring staff and medical facility of the infirmary in developing the confidence in the elderly inmates and maintaining the quality of their social life. Remaining active at this stage is also found to be important for mental health and self-esteem in the elderly persons.

Dr. Sukhendu Debarma in the paper 'Elderly or Old Age People in the Tribal Society of Tripura– A Case Study of the Kokborok Speaking People' attempts to identify how the forces of urbanization, modernization and globalization have affected the status and situation of the elderly persons in the Kokborok speaking tribal society. Here, the author observes that in the traditional tribal society of the Kokborok speaking people of Tripura the elderly or old age people are considered as an asset since time immemorial. In his field study of the Chandithakur para, West Tripura and Dilliram para, South Tripura, it was noticed that elderly or old age people never sit idle. While most of the elderly men remain busy in making baskets of different kinds from bamboo and similar activities elderly women helped out in the kitchen brewing rice beer and looked after their grandchildren or great-grandchildren. But the society has not remained unaffected by the onslaught of modern life and now-a-days, few cases of empty-nest syndrome are found even among the Kokborok speaking people.

In the paper on 'Elderly Persons of Tripura: An Empirical Study' Dr. Anjali Chakraborty attempts to detect the sources of insecurity of the aged persons and suggests some remedies to motivate the government and society. The study explores physical, psychological and socio-economic problems faced by the elderly persons of Tripura.

In a hospital based study to examine the prevalence of coronary heart disease (CHD) and congestive heart failure (CHF) among elderly in Tripura Dr. Atanu Ghosh and Dr. Binapani Doley, carry out a retrospective analysis of 6002 echocardiography reports at G B Hospital, Agartala from 1.1.2002 to 30.9.2006. It is observed that CHD is the most prevalent of all heart diseases in the study group followed by Cardiomyopathy. Both CHD and CHF are essentially serious ailments affecting mainly elderly, which not only determine their quality of life (QOL), but also account for highest mortality in India for all cardiovascular diseases. A Subgroup analysis of age and sex specific prevalence of CHD and CHF finds highest prevalence of CHD (69.7 per cent) in age group 51years and above. Sub Group analysis also revealed a prevalence of 64.7 per cent CHF in elderly age group in Tripura. The male/ female ratio of CHD in elderly is 3:1 Analysis of Left Ventricular Ejection Fraction (EF), which is the most important prognostic criterion of patients as per age and sex are also made. A low EF is associated with low level of QOL and frequent hospitalizations. 49.6 per cent elderly male and 57.9 per cent elderly female CHD patients exhibited below normal EF. Thus the prevalence of both CHD and CHF are very high among elderly in Tripura. The study observes that elderly female tend to have a more malignant course. The study emphasizes the role of life course experiences in determining the health condition during the later stages of life and attempts to explain the high prevalence (22.4 per cent) of the coronary diseases in Tripura which is comparable to results available from Amritsar (22 per cent) and Chandigarh (24 per cent), in terms of high proportion of displaced persons in the region. The study also suggests measures for control and management of the disease.

The Study of the Health Aspect of Elderly at Sandhyanir-Bridhyashram at Gandhi Gram, was carried out among the elderly people of "Sandhya Nir, Gandhigram, during the year 2006 with an aim to determine the rural urban location, age, sex, the treatment seeking, disability, psychological distress and medical problems of all the subjects of Sandhyanir. This cross sectional study of elderly persons in the old age home reveals that while 93 per cent of them do not have any psychological distress, 70 per cent are having moderate disability. The commonest health problems of the elderly are visual impairment (73 per cent), hearing declination (63 per cent) and hypertension (53 per cent) respectively.

In his article 'Geriatric Medical Services in Tripura: Today, Tomorrow and Day-after' Dr. Sushanta Kumar Sen stresses the fact that the elderly population has become a significant group of population with special health care needs, as their number and proportion has increased to a large extent due to life expectancy gains. He identifies the health problems faced by the aged and suggests short and long term measures to equip the health care delivery system of Tripura to meet the emerging needs of the elderly population.

In the empirical study of old-age-related problems and programmes, Dr. Dhanajoy Gan Choudhury reviews the existing and ever-growing literature on gerontology in order to study the local issues. He focuses on the efforts of different individuals in Tripura who are trying to make a difference in the lives of the elderly persons here. He emphasizes the importance of imparting traditional values of Indian culture in order to facilitate proper integration of the aged in society.

Mr Harekrishna Chakraborty and Ms Kalyani Bhattacharya, the social activists of this tiny state observed that the elderly people used to hold a respectable position and were given due honour in the surroundings of joint family system. Both of them felt the need of popularizing the practice of special health care needs of this vulnerable category of the population and also recommended some suggestive measures for the improvement of the situation.

The issues of social security of the elderly persons are addressed in Social Security of Old Age Persons in Rural Areas: An Empirical Study by Jayanta Choudhury. The author not only elaborates on the concept of social security and mentions the legal and institutional provisions available for the elderly persons in India but also emphasizes the need for proper implementation of the schemes. In order to monitor the implementation of the schemes he develops an indicator and suggests different measures. On the basis of a field study he concludes that the implementation of the National Old Age Pension Scheme has been satisfactory in Tripura.

The paper 'Socio-economic Status of the Elderly People: A Case Study of Malabati Tea Estate of Tripura, by Partha Sengupta brings out the conditions of the elderly persons who earned their living as daily workers in the tea estate. The description of their actual life situation presented in the case studies underscores the unmet need for support from the employers, government and non-government organizations in order to improve their quality of life.

Poverty and declining health emerges as the two major problems in the lives of the elderly persons, which needs attention. Generating opportunities for the elderly individuals to lead an active life, so that they can add to the household income is a challenge requiring focus and intensive research. Proper modification and adjustment in health infrastructure to cope up with the growing number of elderly population has to be designed according to the lines suggested in the contributions in this volume.

We are grateful to the Director, Indian Council of Social Science Research, North Eastern Regional Centre (ICSSR-NERC) who proposed the idea of holding seminar on 'the magnitude of the problems of elderly persons of Tripura' and also sponsored the same. We are also thankful to the Women's Study Cell, Tripura University for extending their cooperation for organizing this State Level Seminar.

Chandrika Basu Majumder
&
Paramita Saha

Contributors

Dr. Anjali Chakraborty, Reader, Department of Political Science, MBB College, Agartala

Dr. Arun Ghosh, Tutor, Department of Microbiology, AGMC & G B Hospital, Agartala

Dr. Atanu Ghosh, I/C. Echo Lab, Nodal Officer Telemedicine, AGMC & G B Hospital Agartala

Dr. Beenapani Doley, Professor and Head, Department of Medicine, AGMC & G B Hospital, Agartala

Dr. Chandrika Basu Majumder, Head, Department of Political Science, Tripura University, Agartala

Dr. Dhananjoy Gan Choudhury, Reader, Department of Political Science, M B B College.

Harekrishna Chakraborty, Social Activist, Agartala

Mr. Jayanta Choudhury, Sr. Lecturer, Centre for Rural Studies, Tripura University

Ms Paramita Saha, Lecturer, Department of Applied and Analytical Economics, Tripura University.

Mr. Partha Sengupta, Social Activist, Agartala

Professor Satyadeo Poddar, Department of History, Tripura University.

Dr. Sukhendu Debbarma, Reader and Head, Department of History. Tripura University

Dr. Susanta Sen, AGMC and G B Hospital, Agartala

Key Note Address

—Binoytosh Dutta

The partition of the Country did immense damage to the social fabric of two areas of the then undivided India, one Bengal and the other Punjab. The uprooted Bengalis from East Pakistan for the safety of their life crossed borders in the Eastern part adjoining Tripura, Assam and other bordering states. These helpless people left behind all their landed properties, business and professions in which they were engaged.

Family was the worst victim – all the kith and kins were separated in many cases. The cohesive society in which they had been living through generations was suddenly eliminated and they like water-hyacinths floated for an unknown and uncertain future. The rough and tough battle for existence began. But not the comfort and easiness of a warm family life surrounded by near relatives who have long been bound by blood relations.

That was a traumatic experience for the victims who were forced to leave their ancestral life and soil for an unknown destination chartering a rough sea for a new shelter. With that also began the uncertainty of old age. In the new situation the parents struggled hard to rear their children – the joint family conception gradually disappeared and the nucleus families became the role model, a beckoning for a solitary life for the elderly people, especially the parents. The horizon of a gloomy and brooding future loomed large. With a powerful onslaught of globalization the old tree of joint family life was completely uprooted – elderly person became alive– the children in search of better job prospects left their families for a brighter future. Occasionally they would visit their parents "fell upon the thorns of life" they bled. They were undone –a bleak future for then- the warmth of family life with children, grandchildren everything disappeared– it was so shocking. But helpless they were destined to be. The nuclear family spectre right about the family fabric irrespective of caste, religion, educated and uneducated, the rich and the poor.

Some suggest Old Age Home as a panacea. But nothing can be a substitute for a dear home. The longing of the elderly person for their sons and daughters, the grandchildren can not be replaced by anything; they crave for warmth, the smiles and giggles of the helpless grand-sons and daughters.

Outstretching the boundary the wide world outside has no respect or regard for the helpless. In all situations, whether in governmental or social establishments the elderly persons are hardly cared for, better not to expect a gentle and a respectful attitude. The elderly persons have been crowned with a mouthful of a phrase "senior citizens" – on what a greeting then get from the junior ones in all situations! Promises and promises –but nothing tangible anywhere. To wait of a little list of whatever governmental concessions there are one is to run from pillar to post –no helping hands greet them. Health care is absent. When the senior citizen requires medical facilities, the most they do not get any. Prices of essential drugs are rising by leaps and bounds, from my own experience I can assert that it becomes a burden for most of the retired employees and a mirage for the elderly persons who lived below poverty level. No concerted move is there from the administration, ministries, whether central or state governments. The lip service is the practice of the day. Excuses of fund crunch is a shield for them to hide there worthless rule to reign the country or run the administration. How much money is spent for the bureaucrats for their travels throughout the length and breadth of this poor country? Only in a few states in India something tangible has been done for the elderly persons elsewhere it is only a long list of promises – for the elderly persons it is a nightmare. The government and the NGO's have no commitment – they only look for media propaganda.

That's all money problem of the elderly persons can be solved if all of us feel for each other, bear in mind that everyone of us shall become elderly people one day. We require a determined will and a selfless dedication caring for the offices of profit. Let "service before self" be our motto.

The magnitudes of the problem of elderly persons are many and varied. When a great number of people of our state live below poverty line and when funds for their enlistment are not sufficient, where two morsels of food is what they need, that can also be met up. Where hunger and deprivation is the rule of the day who thinks about the elderly people of this level? Magnitude of the problems of the elderly persons cannot be discussed in the isolation of the general economic conditions of the state. The number of persons begging for a livelihood has come down but underneath lies a sad and inconsolable situation of helpless grey heads!

To make short of this long discourse of the key address I apprehend that the growing menace of globalization and consumerism of our small state Tripura, shall also not be spared. Beside the glittering lights of the cities and towns the darkness of the remote areas where people of all communities are fighting a grim battle of survival, we shall have to take account of the vacant looks of the elderly persons, proper health care system and the magic touch of their of eyes shining with love and compassion –the like of Mother Teressa who single handedly provided shelter to the destitute children and the frail elderly person, appearing as a Saviour.

1

The Added Years of Life – Elderly Women in Tripura

—Paramita Saha

Introduction

Increased life expectancy has been a major success story of modern times. Following effective biomedical research there are new possibilities of retarding the process of ageing of an individual. However, this has resulted in population ageing i.e. increase in the proportion of elderly persons in total population. The proportion of elderly population in Tripura (70.27%, Census, 2001) is highest among the north eastern states. The figure is even higher than the national average.

Often statistical information on older populations is grouped into a broad open category '60 years and over', which obscures the heterogeneous nature of the population group, identified as the elderly population. Age and gender subgroups within this sub-population can have a very different survival experiences, quite apart from interrelated differences traceable to social class, education, income, lifestyle health and regional aspects. The older world is increasingly a female world.

As is the experience world over, in the added years of their life, number of elderly women exceeds that of the elderly males. In Tripura also elderly women outnumber elderly men. It is observed that the situation of the elderly males and elderly females differ to a great extent. It is common knowledge that ageing brings more miseries to women than men. Discourses on elderly population cannot therefore, remain oblivious to the problems and needs of the increasing number and proportion of elderly women. The present paper thus focuses on the gender dimensions of the elderly population. The major purpose is to find out the actual condition of the elderly women in Tripura based on the information gathered from households with elderly members.

The present analysis is based on primary data collected from a household survey originally devised for a comprehensive study on Population Ageing in Tripura, held during September 2003 to November 2004. The census data for different years provide an idea about the number and growth of elderly female population. The detailed information on the livelihood issues of the elderly women in Tripura is obtained through a multistage sample survey conducted in eight villages and two municipal areas selected purposively from West District and South District. The sample consisted of 308 elderly respondents (149 male and 159 female) selected randomly from the households with elderly members in chosen urban and rural areas. A structured questionnaire is used to collect the information through direct interview of the elderly males and females. The information is presented in a tabular form. Comparative analysis of the situation of the elderly women vis-à-vis elderly men are done on the basis of indicators in the form of different rates, ratios and proportions.

The paper is divided into three sections. A brief introduction to the problem and the scope, objective and methodology are discussed in Section I. Findings from the Census data are presented in Section II. The survey data are analysed in Section III highlighting the differences in the living conditions, economic situation and health conditions of the elderly males and elderly females.

II

Demographic Profile of Elderly Women

As population grows over time the age structure also undergoes changes, raising the absolute number of the elderly persons, as well as their proportion in the population (Table 1). The pattern of increase of elderly population and of elderly males and elderly females as reflected in the census figures are also presented in Table 1. Disaggregating elderly population of different census years according to gender reveals that number of elderly female in total elderly population of Tripura has increased steadily over time and in 2001, elderly females have outnumbered their male counterpart. While the elderly population has been increasing, in each census year the growth rate of elderly females has remained higher than that of elderly males (Table 2).

In this context the proportion of elderly females in the elderly population, and proportion of elderly females among female population may be considered. As the growth rate of elderly females has always remained higher than that of elderly males the proportion of elderly females in elderly population has become 51.55 per cent in 2001(Table 3). This conforms to the global experience that the female share increases over time and is termed as 'feminisation of the elderly' (Dhar Chakraborty, 2004). Moreover, the proportion of the elderly females among female population of Tripura has been increasing steadily over the years. In contrast the proportion of elderly among the male population shows a decline both in 1991 and 2001 (Table 3). This reflects greying of the female population.

Table 1
Elderly Population of Tripura (1961-2001)

Year	*Elderly Male*	*Elderly Female*	*Total Elderly*
1961	33522	28365	61887 (5.42)
1971	55192	47276	102468 (6.58)
1981	75358	69372	144730 (7.05)
1991	97939	95356	193295 (7.01)
2001	112656	119893	232549 (7.27)

Source: Census of India, Socio-cultural Tables, 1961, 1971, 1981, 1991, Age - data 2001, RGCCI, New Delhi.

Note: Figures in the parentheses are percentages of elderly population in total population in respective years.

Table 2
Annual Average Growth Rate of Population in Tripura

(in per cent)

Year	*Total Population*	*Elderly population*	*Elderly Male*	*Elderly Female*
1961-71	3.62	6.55	6.46	6.66
1971-81	3.19	4.12	3.65	4.67
1981-91	3.42	3.35	2.99	3.74
1991-01	1.60	2.03	1.50	2.57

Source: Same as Table 1.

Table 3
Greying of Female Population in Tripura

Year	*Proportion of Elderly Female in elderly population (in percent)*	*Proportion of Elderly Female in female population (in percent)*	*Proportion of Elderly Male in male population (in percent)*	*Elderly Sex Ratio***	*Overall Sex ratio**
1961	45.83	5.15	5.66	846	932
1971	46.13	6.25	6.88	856	943
1981	47.93	6.94	7.14	920	946
1991	49.33	7.12	6.90	973	945
2001	51.55	7.70	6.85	1064.	948

Source: Census of India, Socio-Cultural Tables, 1961, 1971, 1981, 1991, Age-data 2001, RGCCI, New Delhi.

Note: * Female per thousand male in total population.

**Elderly female per thousand elderly male.

Thus, it may be concluded that ageing of female population is more pronounced. Sex ratio is often taken as a summary indicator of status of women in a society and an improvement in the sex ratio, as an indicator of improvement in their status. The elderly sex ratio (number of elderly females per thousand elderly males) is of great interest as it indicates the differential mortality in the two sexes (Dandekar, 1996). The elderly sex ratio in Tripura, has improved continuously since 1961 and has remained above the overall sex ratio since 1981(Table 3). It may be noted here that the elderly sex ratio (1064) in Tripura is even higher than that of Kerala (1058) as per the 2001 Census figures.

The urban and rural areas are considered separately in Table 4. It is observed that even though elderly sex ratio in the urban area remained favourable to females, it has been decreasing over the years1981, 1991 and 2001. In contrast, the rural elderly sex ratio improved continuously over the years and became favourable to the rural elderly females in 2001. In 2001 number of elderly females per 1000 elderly males in the rural area has become 1047.

Table 4
Elderly Persons in Rural and Urban Areas of Tripura

Elderly	*1981*		*1991*		*2001*	
	Rural	*Urban*	*Rural*	*Urban*	*Rural*	*Urban*
Male	68189	7169	84358	13581	93023	19633
Female	61566	7806	79651	15705	97478	22415
Total	129755	14975	164009	29286	190501	42048
Sex Ratio	902	1088	944	1156	1047	1141

Source: same as in Table 1.

These findings point to the fact that females have higher life expectancy at birth and lower mortality (Rajan et al 1999). These also indicate long-term improvements in female survival at later ages in the life. While in the urban area this has been evident for a longtime, in the rural area also the improving sex ratio indicate improved life expectancy. This is a universal phenomenon, experienced worldwide which is likely to continue in future also. The implication is that both in rural and urban areas, the life conditions for females have improved resulting in increased presence of women in the older age group.

The increasing presence of women in the elderly population, higher growth rate of elderly females compared to elderly males implies that many of the elderly women will be widows. The marital status happens to be an important determinant of the social and economic status of the elderly females, particularly when they are not educated and do not have any income or property. Marital status of the elderly population as reflected in the census data are provided in Table 5.

Table 5
Marital Status Elderly Population of Tripura in 2001

Proportion	*Male*	*Female*	*Total*
Married	86.58	39.07	62.0
Widowed	11.24	58.96	35.85

Source: Age-data 2001, RGCCI, New Delhi.

Note: Never- married and divorced/-separated categories are not shown because of their small proportion.

While 86.58 per cent of the elderly males are currently married, only 39.07 per cent of females in the in the elderly category are married. Compared to the males, a much higher proportion of elderly females are widows (58.96 per cent).

Such gender disparity in widowhood arises because of the convention of marrying women to older men. Also men are more likely to remarry and are able to maintain the currently married status for a longer part of their life. Moreover, the female life expectancy at birth has increased more than that of males, meaning females live longer. Divergence of life expectancy between the sexes has important implications with regard to the living arrangements, economic conditions and health of older persons as the survey data reveal.

III

Socio-economic and Health conditions of Elderly Women

The socio-economic characteristics of the sample elderly persons are presented in Table 6. It shows that the proportion of elderly females is higher among rural elderly population (55 per cent) compared to the urban elderly (47 per cent). The census data presented in Table 4 shows a decline in elderly sex ratio in the urban areas from 1991 to 2001. The survey findings confirm that there is a tendency of falling elderly sex ratio in the urban area.

Proportion elderly females in the below poverty line (BPL) elderly population is higher than that among above poverty line (APL) elderly population. The proportion of females in the elderly population of ST community (47 per cent) is lower than that in the non-

ST community. The literacy rate of the elderly females (42 per cent) is much lower than that of the elderly males (79 per cent).

Table 6
Socio-economic Profile of the Elderly Persons

No. of Elderly	Male	Female	Total
In rural areas	81 (45)	99 (55)	180 (100)
In urban areas	68 (53)	60 (47)	128(100)
BPL	**49(39.5)**	**75 (60.5)**	**124**
APL	**100(54.3)**	**84(45.7)**	**184**
ST	35	31	66
SC	16	17	33
Others	98	111	209
Illiterates	**31(21)**	**92(58)**	**123(39)**
Literates	**118(79)**	**67(42)**	**185(61)**
Owner of house	125	53	178
Do not own house	24	106	130
Age below 70 yrs	**67**	**73**	**140**
Age above 70 yrs	**82**	**86**	**168**

Source: Field survey.
Note: The figures in parentheses show percentages.

Living arrangements of the elderly women

The most commonly used indicators to describe the living arrangements of the elderly persons, are proportion of persons living alone, co-residence rate, and headship ratio. Loneliness in old age is a painful fact of life. In extreme situation this may take the form of elderly persons living alone. A cross-country study of living arrangements of elderly persons in the developing world covering Africa, Asia and Latin America (Bongaarts and Zimmer, 2001) reports 8.8 per cent of older individuals living alone across all countries and the average proportion of living alone is nearly twice as high for women. Data from the present survey shows that, 14.5 per cent of the elderly women in the sample live alone as against only 2 per cent of elderly men living alone (Table 7).

Table 7
Elderly Persons Living Alone

	No. of Elderly persons	*Living alone*	*Per cent Living alone*
Male	149	3	2
Female	159	23	14.5
Female Urban	60	10	16.7
Female Rural	99	13	13.1
Widow	118	23	19.5
Widower	23	2	8.7

Source: Field Survey

The vulnerability of elderly women across countries is indeed striking. The probability, that an elderly woman will live alone, increases with the death of husband. All the elderly women who are found to be living alone happened to be widows and among the elderly widows the proportion of living alone is as high as 19.5 per cent.

However, the survey reveals that co-residence is the dominant form of living arrangement for the elderly persons in Tripura, the co-residence rate being 857 per thousand (Table 8). Co-residence is crucial in determining the economic conditions of the elderly persons as co-residence enables the elderly person to have a higher income entitlement.

Table 8
Co-residence Rate among Elderly Males and Females

Persons	*Co-resident*	*Total*	*Co-residence Rate*
Male	132	149	885
Female	132	159	830
Total	264	308	857

Source: Field survey

However, among the elderly women co-residence rate is lower compared to that among elderly men implying that more women compared to men are likely to live separately from their children in their old age.

A majority (59.7 per cent) of elderly respondents reported that they are the heads of their households (Table 9). But considerable gap exists in the female and male headship ratio, calculated as the ratio of number of head of the household to total population in the group.

Table 9
Marital Status of Head of Household (HoH)

Marital Status	*Male HoH*	*Female HoH*	*Total*
Married	109	5	114
Widowed	18	52	70
Total	127(0.85)	57(0.36)	184(59.7)

The female headship ratio (0.36) is much lower than the male headship ratio (0.85). Among the 57 female heads of household 52 are found to be widows, indicating that women are elevated to the status of head of the household only after the death of their husbands. This is not to mean that all women become heads of household at their husbands' death. Only 44 per cent of all elderly widowed women are head of households. Headship ratio among those elderly who have a regular source of income (0.70) is higher than those who do not have any regular income (0.52). Thus a regular source of income helps the elderly persons to maintain their status as heads of household. However, lower headship ratio among them is only to be expected as elderly women rarely have a regular source of income.

Economic condition of the elderly women

The higher proportion of elderly females in the BPL category (Table 6) suggests poverty afflicts elderly women relatively more. Proportions of elderly women, who are widows, are illiterate and are not owner of their houses is higher than those among male elderly. All these indicate the lower socioeconomic status of elderly females and their greater vulnerability in old age. Only 37 per cent of the sample elderly females are found to have a regular source of income.

Participation in the workforce by the elderly may be interpreted in two very different ways. On one hand this may be seen as a prolongation of working life due to improvements in health conditions. As opposed to this, working till late years in life may also mean lack of lifetime savings and other sources of financial support.

Table 10
Work Participation Rate of the Elderly Population in Tripura

Proportion of Main Workers Among Elderly			
Year	*Male*	*Female*	*Total*
1981	65.00	5.70	36.73
1991	63.14	6.97	35.43
2001	57.07	8.94	32.26
India 2001	60.25	20.93	40.31

Source: Economic Tables, Census of India, 1981, 1991, and 2001.

The work participation rate of elderly female has always remained lower than that of elderly male. But work participation rate of elderly females shows an upward trend (increasing by 56 per cent from 5.70 in 1981 to 8.94 in 2001, Table 10) While proportion of elderly males in male main workers has declined over the years, proportion of elderly females in female main workers has increased (Table 11) by 35 percent in twenty years from 1981 to 2001. One pertinent question is if labour market is biased against elderly men, how is it that proportion of elderly females in female main workers going up? One possibility is, elderly women seek work in desperate conditions and are ready to work for a lower wage, and in a low status jobs for example as housemaids where males are not suitable.

Increased participation of elderly women in the labour market indicates their deteriorating economic situation and inadequate support structure and economic vulnerability of the elderly women.

Table 11
Elderly Workers in Tripura

Proportion of Elderly Workers in Main Workers of All Ages			
Year	*Male*	*Female*	*Total*
1981	9.44	4.64	8.70
1991	9.28	4.90	8.53
2001	8.66	6.29	8.22

Source: Economic Tables, Census of India, 1981, 1991, and 200

While 44 per cent of elderly males have some regular financial support from public or social security sources only 36 per cent of female elderly has access to such sources.

Even when the elderly women have some income they have little control over it. Most of the time, the children with whom they are staying, handle these. One widow in the urban area earning family pension said that it is her son who collects the pension after she signs the papers and takes care of all her needs. Should she need any cash she has to ask for it, which she dislikes to do, though her son rarely refuses. She says she does not have any other alternative because by giving up the control over the pension she is actually ensuring that she would be looked after. Several similar cases are found where the direction of intra household transfer of fund is reversed in order to ensure reciprocal behaviour in future. This type of parent to child transfers may be interpreted as informal arrangements for services that do not have a well-developed market.

Health of elderly women

Personal health is a priority concern in old age as ability to work is contingent upon physical health. Illness in old age is an ever-present threat to the means of self-support. Thus, health is one of the most important components of well being in the later life. The subjective feeling of the elderly persons about their health is an important issue in studies analyzing the health situation of the elderly. To many elderly persons ill health in old age is but a natural phenomenon.

An indicator of health status is essential for a comparative analysis and for prioritizing of health care initiatives and allocation of health care funds. But a universally acceptable health status index has remained elusive due to unavailability of data and other conceptual difficulties (Srinivasan, 1998). For the present purpose morbidity rates and hospitalisation rates are considered, (Table 12) which are estimated as

$$\textbf{Morbidity Rate} = \frac{\text{Number of persons who had fallen sick during 15 days prior to the survey requiring treatment}}{\text{Total population at risk during the same period.}} \times 1000$$

$$\textbf{Hospitalisation Rate} = \frac{\text{Number of persons hospitalized in the one year prior to the survey}}{\text{Total population at risk during the same period.}} \times 1000$$

One inevitable feature of older life is the difficulties faced in movement, in performing activities of daily life and manual work. The data in this regard is shown in Table 13.

Table 12
Health Conditions of Elderly Persons

Elderly Persons	*Proportion feeling unhealthy (per 1000)*	*Morbidity rate*	*Hospitalisation rate*
Male	540	255	161
Female	600	251	119
Total	571	253	139

Source: Field Survey.

Table 13
Difficulties faced by Elderly Persons

No. of persons facing difficulties in	*Male*	*Female*	*Total*
Movement	52 (34.9)	93 (58.5)	145 (47.1)
Daily Activities	27 (18.1)	38 (23.9)	65 (21.1)
Manual Work	69 (46.3)	91 (57.2)	160 (51.9)
No complain	57 (38.2)	29 (18.2)	86 (27.9)

Source: Field Survey.

Note: Figures in the parentheses denote percentages of number of respondents in each group. As respondents often reported to be facing multiple difficulties the per centages do not add up to 100.

Table 12 shows that the proportion of persons feeling unhealthy among elderly females is higher compared to proportion of elderly males feeling unhealthy. A higher proportion of elderly females compared to elderly males are found to face difficulty in movement, in performing daily activities and manual work (Table 13).

Though proportionately more elderly women felt unhealthy, the morbidity rate and hospitalization rate are higher among elderly males indicating that comparatively fewer elderly females have access to treatment in illness.

The vulnerability of elderly women has to be addressed with reference to the adversities faced in the earlier part of life. Ingrained and structural inequalities in early life are viewed as contributory factors to the poor health and poor quality of life in the old age. A change in the age structure is accompanied by changes in disease pattern from acute communicable diseases to chronic diseases of old age. Individual behavioural changes for prevention and treatment become important in such cases of chronic diseases. The emphasis is more on management rather than cure. Funding patterns and health care infrastructure also need rearrangements to address the issue of increasing prevalence of chronic diseases.

In planning for the future health care needs of the elderly, it will be useful to take into account the proportions of aged men and women, who are alone, widowed, non- co-resident rather than elderly age proportions as such. Increased proportion of elderly people living alone will require more formal care and support.

REFERENCES

Bongaarts, J. and Z. Zimmer (2001) "Living Arrangements of Older Adults in the Developing World: An Analysis of DHS Household

Surveys". Population Council, Policy Research Division Working Paper No.148:1-30.

Dandekar, Kumudini (1996): *The Elderly in India.* New Delhi, Sage Publications India Pvt. Ltd.

Dhar Chakraborty, Rajagopal (2004): *The Greying of India, Population Ageing in the Context of Asia.* New Delhi, Sage Publications.

Rajan, S.I., U.S. Mishra and P. Sankara Sarma (1999) *India's Elderly: Burden or Challenge?* New Delhi, Sage Publications India Pvt. Ltd.

Srinivasan, K. (1998) *Basic Demographic Technique and Applications.* New Delhi, Sage Publications India Pvt. Ltd.

2

Problem of Loneliness Among the Elderly Persons of Tripura

—Satyadeo Poddar

Conception of Elderly Persons

There are two approaches widely prevalent to deal with the demarcation of elderly persons, one is calendar age and another is biological age. Many developed countries have adopted the chronological age of 65 years as a definition of elderly persons, but the present study is based on the report of UN where it has been accepted an elderly person who has completed 60 years. According to P. Gorman, "The ageing is of course a biological reality which has its own dynamic, largely beyond human control". However, it is also subject to the constructions by which each society makes sense of old age. In the developed world, chronological time plays a paramount role. The age of 60 or 65, roughly equivalent to retirement age in most developed countries is said to be the beginning of old age. In many parts of the developing world, chronological time has no importance in the meaning of the old age. Other socially constructed meanings of age are more significant such as the roles assigned to older people, in some cases it is the loss of roles accompanying physical decline which is significant in defining old age."

Indian conception of elderly persons in history

In Indian scriptures, the definition of old age is found. Manu divided the whole span of life into four stages: Brahmacharya or celibacy came first; then it was grihastha or householder (when a person is expected to shoulder the responsibility of a citizen and discharge debts to parents by begetting children), next came vanaprastha (which entailed giving up worldly pursuits in order to follow spiritual growth by leaving home for the forest) and the final stage was Sanyasa or renunciation and asceticism. Vanaprastha thus indicated old age- winding down social obligations.

Loneliness as a vital problem

There are many problems which come naturally in the process of old age and one vital problem of old age is loneliness. The nature of loneliness which younger generation talks about in a romantic style is not exactly synonymous to the loneliness which comes in old age. The loneliness can make one feel unloved and unwanted and socially inadequate. Loneliness gives birth to self –consciousness and makes the aged feel ill at ease with others. Loneliness is sometimes expressed in anger and in being critical about others. In a simple language, elderly persons come to such stage where they are living in a society but they do not feel part of it. One is in crowd but not the part of it. When feeling of relations and belongingness is lost, loneliness enters into the life of elderly people.

Despite the historical-cultural tradition of care and respect for the elderly persons along with Governmental and Non-Governmental initiatives, the problems of the elderly persons which remained unsolved or least solved is the problem of loneliness. Loneliness is an emotional state in which a person experiences a powerful feeling of emptiness and isolation. A study conducted by the Centre for Cognitive and Social Neuroscience at University of Chicago in 2006 found loneliness can add 30 points to a blood pressure reading for adults over the age of 50 years. The study of nature of loneliness among the elderly people of Tripura has been taken up in this background.

Bahadur Shah Zafar, who had been proclaimed as an emperor of India, was overthrown by the British. He was arrested from Humayun's tomb, where he was hiding with his three sons and a grandson. Captain Hosdon killed his sons and grandson and their several heads were brought before him. Bahadur Shah was tried for treachery. He was exiled to Rangoon, Burma (now Myanmar), in 1858 where he lived his last five years and died in 1862. While in prison, a sense of loneliness which Zafar felt can be expressed in his own poem:

Lagataa Nahii. n Hai Jii Merra Uja.De Dayaar me.n
Kis Kii Banii Hai aalam-e-naa paayedaar me.n
Kah do in hasarato.n se kahii.n aur jaa base.n
Itanii jagah kahaa.N hai dil-e daaG daar me.n
Umr-e-daraaz maa.Ng kar laaye chaar din
Do arazuu me.n kaT gaye do intazaar me.in
Kitnaaa hai bad nasiib "zafar" dafn ke liye
Do gaz zamiin bhii na milii kuu-e-yaar me.in

National Policy for Older Persons

Since 1992, India had promoted the welfare for the elderly persons throughout the nationwide network of non-governmental organizations and have set up and run old age homes and day care centre, mobile Medicare and other non-institutional services. National Policy for Old Person (NPOP) came into being in 1999, with the primary objective to encourage individuals to make provision for their own as well as their spouse's old age, to encourage families to take care of their older family members, to enable and support voluntary and non-governmental organizations, to promote research and training facilities to train geriatric care givers and organizers of the services for the elderly. In this regard the union Government financed 90 per cent expenditure of non-governmental organizations. Voluntary organizations financed by the government appointed social workers to help the elderly people in legal, banking and tax matters, and in getting access to medical facilities

Growth of Elderly Population in India and Tripura

Demographic ageing is a global phenomenon. With a comparatively young population, India is still poised to become home to the second number of older persons in the world. Projection studies indicate that the number of 60+ in India will increase to 100 million in 2013 and to 198 million in 2030. The UN defines a country as 'aging ' where the proportion of people over 60 reaches 7 per cent. India has already exceeded this and is likely to reach 12.6 per cent by 2025. The special features of the elderly population in India are: a) majorities (80 per cent) of them are in the rural areas, thus making service delivery a challenge. (b) feminization of the elderly population (51per cent of the elderly population would be women by the year 2016), (c) increase in the number of the older-old(persons above 80 years) and (d) a large per centage(30 per cent) of the elderly are below the poverty line. Over and above, a large portion of aged is that of widows and widowers. The proportion of widowers is almost three times less than that of widows.

Table 1
Increasing strength of Elderly Persons in India

Year	*Total population of aged people in India*
1971	28 million
1981	42 million
1991	56 million
2001	75 million
2025	175 + (expected)
2050	324 (expected)

Of the 193.1 million households (excluding institutional households) at the national level enumerated at the 2001 Census, about 58.3 million or 30.2 per cent of households are reported to have at least one elderly persons (60 years and above) as member of the household whereas, also 21.3 per cent of the households have recorded one elderly person as member, the proportion of households with two elderly persons was 8.4 per cent. The proportion of households with three or more elderly persons was a meager 0.5 per cent. The rural-urban differential is apparent with higher proportion of elderly population reported from rural households compared to urban households. The following data shows the numerical strength of elderly persons in Tripura

Table 2

Elderly Households in Tripura

Total number of households	663662
Number of households with no Aged Persons	472607
Household with one aged Person	145284
Number of single member household	7656
Aged male members in single member household	2053
Aged female members in single member household	5603
Sex ratio of single member aged households	2729
Percentage of single member aged households to households with one aged person	5.3

Table 3

Elderly Persons at a Glance, 2001

No. of Elderly Persons in India	77 million
Elderly Persons living in rural areas	75 % of the total population
No. of women elderly persons	48.2 % of the total population
No of Elderly women who are widow	55 % of the total population
No. of Elderly Persons who are illiterate & dependent on physical labour	73 % of the total population
No. of Elderly Persons living below the poverty line	one third of the total population
No. of Elderly Persons living just above poverty line	66 % of older persons
No. of Elderly Persons working in unorganized sector (4*)	90 % of the total population

Source: http://www.helpageindia.com/

Concept of Loneliness

Indian society has been providing the best place for the satisfaction of physical and emotional comfort for the elderly people. The extended family system, strong kinship and religious values are the corner-stone of the Indian social system and this act as a natural social security for old people. This security of the elderly persons flowed from their superior status in the family and by virtue of the fact, that the elderly persons enjoyed considerable status in the family, particularly over family property. This ensured their dominance in the family, and in turn, the children had to care of their aging parents as an obligation and as a sign of reverence. The family structure of Tripura is largely based on the age long concept of natural social security which Indian tradition has been providing to the old people. In contrast to it, the new industrial social order of India, which is marked by industrialisation, urbanization, secularization and change in women's position, the position of elderly persons has turned very low. Recently, there has been marked change in the treatment of the elderly as compared to the earlier periods. A recent study says that the change is due to transition in the role and status of the elderly persons from pre-industrial society to the existing industrial social order. They say that elderly persons enjoyed a much higher status in pre-industrial society which was marked by group-oriented social interaction, agricultural mode of production, extended family system, kinship and patriarchal authority. In this kind of social situation, conflict and problems of adjustment has become a normal feature of the Indian families. Many of the elderly parents are compelled to leave their children and stay in old homes. Elderly persons are habituated with the feeling care and protection in the extended family and they find it difficult to the environment of old home and therefore leads to the growth of loneliness and depression.

As the traditional role of the family is being shared by institutions such as old homes it is often assumed, and sometimes, argued, that the absence of familial care and surroundings induce feelings of loneliness among the residents of old homes. This study conducted in the old age institution of State Infirmary, Government of Tripura, Narsigarh, Agartala seeks to understand the experience of loneliness. This has been examined with reference to the concepts of 'social loneliness' and 'desolation' advanced by Weiss and Townsend respectively. In this paper, I have tried to examine the activity theory of aging, which links engagement in activities with physical and mental health and self-esteem of the elderly.

In order to deal with this problem, I have taken into account the concept of "Social isolation", "Social loneliness" and "Emotional loneliness". Townsend distinguished between social isolation and desolation in old age. Desolation means having an unwelcome feeling of lack or loss of companionship. It can be caused by the death or illness of the company of someone one loves. Townsend argues that though the two phenomena are related, it is desolation rather isolation that cause loneliness in old age.

The concept of Townsend goes parallel to the concept of social and emotional loneliness of Weiss. Emotional loneliness results from the lack of a close, intimate attachment to another person. Divorced and widows may have such form of loneliness. On the other hand social loneliness is due to the lack of social relationship in which the person is a part of a group of friends who share common interests and activities. Individuals who have recently moved to a new social environment (to a new city, job or college) may go through this type of loneliness. Old persons, who go to old homes, may experience this type of loneliness.

I have tried to look at the activity theory of aging which propounds that engaging in some kind of activity or work, facilitates old people to adjust and alter years of their life and also helps them in avoiding loneliness. Havighurst propounded this theory who contends that there is a positive correlation between activity, mental and social adjustment. He holds that the role crisis created by retirement is overcome by absorbing new roles. In other words, people cannot be happy unless they stay socially active. I have tried to examine whether remaining in activity has a positive correlation with reduction of loneliness of the elderly persons of old age homes.

Setting and Method

For the purpose of this study, I have selected an old age home–Institution of State Infirmary, Government of Tripura, Narsingarh, situated 12 kms away from Agartala. The Home was set up by the Department of Social Welfare and Social Education, Govt of Tripura on 1st April, 1961. One Superintendent with a team of officials looks after the inmates of this Home. One Medical Unit along with One Medical Officer is available to look after the health of the aged and infirm inmates. The facilities provided to the inmates of this Home are:

Fooding, clothing thrice in a year and a pair of chappal in a year, regular medical check-up, television for recreation, Musical instruments for performing cultural activities. Food items with nutritive values like meat, fish, and eggs along with vegetables are provided. There is a provision of 200 seats in the State Infirmary. But at present, 60 inmates are being admitted.

Social Groups of Inmates of State Infirmary, Narsingarh

Total Intake	60
S.C	10
Total Intake	60
S.C	10
General	General – 48
S.C. (10)	8 Nos. Female and 2 Nos Male and mostly Das Community
S.T. (2)	S.T. (2) – 2 Nos. Female and belong to Debbarma Community.
General (48)	38 Nos. Female and 10 Nos. Male – Mostly belong to Pal Debnath, Chakraborty, Banerjee and Bhattacherjee community.

The Old Home is divided into 7 blocks viz. Raja Rammohan Block, Vidyasagar, Vivekananda, Rabindranath Tagore, Nibedita, North Block, Kurvey Bhavan(Sick Block). During the session 2002-03, an amount of Rs. 6.89 lacs were utilized for running the Home. Per day expenditure on the inmate is Rs. 30/-. There is one temple of Radha Krishna and Lord Shiva where worship is done by the inmates. Prayers are the daily routine of the inmates of the Home.

A semi-structured interview schedule was used to tap the respondents' experience of loneliness, living condition in the old age home, life satisfaction and family linkage. I also used the simple observation method to collect data on their daily schedule, I met Nava Ram Tripura, Superintendent of the Home and earlier doctor, Sri J.P. Narayan who served that institution for more than 13 years and asked them about its working. Then I talked to some of the elderly residents with a set of questions on 10th November, 2006.

Results and Discussion

1. In the State Infirmary of Tripura, the sex ration of the respondents shows that out of 60 respondents, 48 are female and 12 are males. Mostly they belong to the age group of 65+. Findings show that all the inmates came to the Home from West Tripura District and they are homeless and possess no source of income.
2. India is a caste-based society and in the Home, it is not the upper caste elderly, rather it represents all sections of society which tell the truth that the problem of elderly persons is beyond the caste hierarchy of the society of Tripura.
3. The study also reveals that most of the female respondents are widows or widowed and some of them have children also who are not financially sound and not in a position to keep them in the family. That suggest the notion that some children could keep their parents but they could not.

4. The study also revealed that the majority of the families come from urban settings, i.e West Tripura District. One can surmise that either families in the villages take care of their aged members or the concept of old homes has not yet gained momentum in the countryside.

5. Some respondents have been asked questions regarding the situations which compel them to come to the Old Home. Most of them reported that their disagreement and conflict with sons and daughters-in-law forced them to come here.

6. The inmates were asked a series of questions on their experiences and extent of loneliness. All the respondents, baring few, expressed that they donot feel lonely and depressed in the environment of the old home. In fact, they do not feel isolated from their family members. It was found that in case of some respondents, their children visit once or twice in a month. Even, some residents themselves visit their children. This shows that the elderly residents and their children have not severed their relations with each other, though they found it difficult to stay together. The constant contact with the family members is one of the factors they do not feel social isolation.

7. The inmates of Infirmary are found engaged in the cleaning the premises, doing gardening, planting vegetables in the premises, attending study classes, doing prayer in the evening which get rid of their loneliness. This finding corroborates the assumption of the activity

theory that engaging in various roles not only improves the physical and mental health of the elderly people but also instils in them a sense of self-esteem.

8. The respondents were asked questions about their relations with other residents. Most of them described their relationship as friendly which is also instrumental in reducing their loneliness. One unmarried lady, Jamana Das, who is handicapped, belonged to Melagarh, is a centre of friendly attraction among the inmates. She recites the sermons of *Gita* and takes leading role in the prayer activities. She is always surrounded by all the inmates.

9. When they were asked whether they feel happy at Old Home or at their own home. All replied that old home stay is very comfortable and they do not feel loneliness here.

10. Inmates of Infirmary are brought out with escort to visit Puja pandals during Durga, Kali Puja and that satisfy their religious thrust and they are constantly looked after by the doctor in case of any serious illness. Medical care provides them mental anxiety which occurs during old age. Their death sacraments are religiously performed by the authority of the Infirmary, that also feel the sense lacuna of helplessness and loneliness.

11. Govind Rani Saha (75 yrs) and Gopi Mohan Saha are the only couple and their mutual care and respect for each other give inspiration to every inmate. Their involvement in the service of others

is one of the viable ways for the avoidance of loneliness.

12. After questioning the Superintendent of Infirmary, revealing information was found. Naba Mohan Debbarma, converted Christian from Jirania, whose father was Ram Kumar Debbarma and under whose name, the existing village is named as Ram Kumar Para. It is Naba Mohan Debbarma, only inmate who of Infirmary who could not found Old Home comfortable and he termed Infirmary as prison and he was feeling suffocated and consequently he left the Home.

Conclusion

In the light of above discussion, it can be concluded that the inmates of State Infirmary of Tripura do not feel lonely and depressed being away from home. They are quite satisfied with their life in the Old Age Home and even saying that they are happier here than at home. The residents do not experience either social isolation or desolation. This is due to the occasional visit of their family members to Infirmary. The care of the staff and medical facility of the Infirmary develop confidence in them and their association with religious work makes them feel that they are not spiritually isolated from the home. The activity theory of aging was examined and it was found that busy in various activities is a positive step for the growth of mental health and self-esteem in the elderly persons. It also helped them get rid of loneliness.

It is very difficult to arrive at a generalisation from this study as it draws upon a small number of respondents. Since the study did not look at other types of old age homes as old homes run by voluntary agencies or old homes managed by the government, it is not possible to generalise that elderly residents do not experience loneliness in all old age homes in India. But, one thing is sure, that elderly persons of the Infirmary of Tripura have no feeling of loneliness.

Suggestions

In India, age was not based on numerical addition of years, but an integrated process of learning through experience. Plans and programmes for the elderly people should be looked at as an integral whole, where life-long individual development was fostered. Productive endeavour at later stages in life, greater interpersonal correlations through new communication technologies, a better and greener environment , greater freedom to travel and seeing other civilizations would certainly help make life richer and worth living and there will be least feeling of loneliness among the elderly persons in Tripura. We should think of the society in which the young and the old, the strong and the weak, should obtain equal opportunities for productive contribution, enhanced human relations and fulfillment of aspirations. In the words of S. Radhakrishnan, the second President of India, **"Years may wrinkle the skin; the soul is wrinkled if you give up love and loyalty."**

NOTES & REFERENCES

1. P. Gorman, Development and the rights of older people, 2000.
2. A 'Household' is usually a group of persons who normally live together and make their meals from a common kitchen unless

the exigencies of work prevent any of them from doing so. There may be one member households, two member households or multiple member households. The household is considered to be basic unit in a society for social, economic, political and sociological process. Household is a co-residential socio-economic unit regardless of kinship ties whereas family is a group-membership in which is mainly based on affinal and consaguinal ties.

3. Nature of loneliness during young age is usually related to missing old friends and family finding hard to replace them with substitutes and high expectation from the society and environment.
4. Unorganized sector means no regular source of income.
5. S. Rajan, U.S. Misra and P.S. Sharma, *India's Elderly, Burden or Challenges?* New Delhi, Sage, 1999.
6. Bulletin of State Infirmary, Narsingarh, Agartala.
7. Kumudini Dandekar, *Elderly in India*, Sage, New Delhi, 1996.

3

Elderly People in the Tribal Society of Tripura– A Case Study of the Kokborok Speaking People

—Sukhendu Debbarma

Ageing is becoming a much discussed issue in India in the recent times. This is due to population ageing. What is most disturbing is the change in family and social situation. Elderly or old age cannot be defined exactly because it does not have the same meaning in all societies or countries. In many parts of the world, people are considered elderly or old because of certain changes in their activities or social roles. For example, people may be considered old when they become grand parents or when they begin to do less or different work. In the United States, people are often considered old if they have lived a certain number of years. Many Americans think of 65 as the beginning of old age because United States workers become eligible to retire with full social security benefits at age 65 whereas in India generally it is 60 years. People in the 65-and-over age group are often called senior citizens. The number of persons aged 60 and over is estimated to be 688 million in 2006 and projected to be 2 billion by 2050. By that time the numbers of the older person will be more than the children. According to the Census 1991, in India the elderly person constitute about 7.6 per cent or about 8 million people (*Times of India*, Nov. 29 2006, p.9). India, like many other developing countries in the world, is presently witnessing rapid ageing of its population. The average life expectancy has gone up from 46 years in 1971 to 64 years in 2000. Almost eight out of 10 older people in India live in rural areas. India is still poised to become home to the second largest number of older persons in the world. Projection studies indicate that the number of 60+ in India will increase to 100 million in 2013 and to 198 million in 2030. Populations everywhere are growing older, and the number of persons aged 60+ years or over is expected nearly to triple by 2050. Not only are more people surviving to reach old age, but those who attain old age are living longer than ever before. The increase in the numbers of elderly or old age people is due to advances in nutrition and health care which have extended the period of good health as well as extending the overall life expectancy. India, like many other developing countries in the world, is presently witnessing rapid ageing of its population. Approximately eight out of 10 elderly in India live in rural areas. The Indian society traditionally has followed the joint family system since time immemorial. With the coming of urbanisation, modernisation and globalisation there is a marked change in economic structure, erosion of societal values and the weakening of social institutions such as the joint family. Changes in the family institution and the nuclear family system are increasing to be the norm. Modern life style, professional ambitions and unrealistic expectations brought about challenges in the very institution of marriage and the family. In this changing economic and social milieu, the younger generation is in search for new identities encompassing economic independence and redefined social roles within, as well as outside, the family. The changing economic structure has altogether reduced the dependence of rural families on land, which had at one point of time provided strength to bonds between generations. The traditional sense of duty and obligation of the younger generation towards the older generation is being eroded. In such a situation the elderly or old age generation is caught between the decline in traditional values on the one hand and the absence of an adequate social security system, on the other. The generation gap is another hurdle which makes it difficult for the young and the old to have dialogue on different issues affecting both and creating gaps. Consequently, the misunderstanding between the two group increases and the family as well as the society becomes further disorganized. Elderly in India was never considered as a social problem until recently. In Indian tradition, an individual life span has been divided into four *Ashrams* (stages) namely, *Baramcharya* (learning in the State of Celibacy), *Grahasth* (family life), *Vanprasth* (detached family life) and *Sanyas* (renounced life). It is this last state of life that society accorded highest respect and prestige to an individual. This is why old age home concept is alien to India. Every section of the citizens in any country is considered important and is the same case with the elderly or old age people. The elderly are considered as an asset since time immemorial in any society. However, with the disintegration of traditional joint/extended family structure, the elderly people are losing the safety net of family support. All elderly persons face ageing in the same way but they do not form a homogeneous group and therefore their needs are not the same all over the world. It is pertinent to mention here that the situation of women is particularly disadvantageous due to lack of education, formal training and participation in the economic development. In the absence of the traditional support from the family, the need for alternatives to counteract this change is an urgent need. The inclusion of study of gerontology in the educational curricula will lead a step forward in the proper understanding of the elderly. The majority of the elderly as mentioned earlier in India live in joint families and children feel responsible for taking care of their parents. With increasing population, migration of younger population and changing social and family structures, the situation for elders has become quite precarious or what can be termed as 'Empty-Nest Syndrome'. There is negative stereotype of ageing where elders are regarded as burden on the society. A quantitative and qualitative analysis of the newspaper columns pertaining to images of the elderly and the ageing issues was carried out under the Media Study. It was found that the newspapers were more or less playing a passive role by merely publishing occasional news and articles regarding individuals and events. This indicates the need to take a more proactive approach. By and large the image of the elderly men and women as reflected in advertisements, cartoons or in the editorial text indicates the tendency of stereo-typing this population as elderly and creating an image of them as a burden on society. There seems to be an inadequate effort on focusing on real issues of ageing and the concerns of population ageing. There seems to be little appreciation of the contributions made by the elderly population either in strengthening family, transmitting culture from one generation to another. The social environment is appreciative neither of the rich experience of the elderly nor of the contribution they can make in political and economic decision-making. In the traditional tribal society of the Kokborok speaking people of Tripura, the elderly are considered as an asset since time immemorial. In spite of the marked changes brought about by urbanization, modernization and globalization somewhat the status and situation of the elderly people in the tribal society of the Kokborok speaking people of Tripura have not undergone any significant changes. Tribal society of the Kokborok speaking people of Tripura is to a large extent joint or extended family and the elderly people are cared by the family members. In such system the '***Muikwthar***' i.e., untouched curry is kept aside for the elderly or old age people in case the other members of the family wants to have meal earlier than the elderly people. Their role in the household is very important and indispensable. In my field study of the Chandithakur para, West Tripura and Dilliram para, South Tripura, it was noticed that elderly never sit idle. Most of the elderly men were making baskets of different kinds from bamboo or were working in the nearby house. The elderly women were giving helping hand in the kitchen, brewing rice beer or looking after their grandchildren or great-grandchildren. In the evening most of the elderly people both men and women will be telling stories or folk tales to their grandchildren or great-grandchildren. It is pertinent to mention here that they also advice their grandchildren or great-grandchildren about dos and don'ts. At the same time it was also noticed that elderly of these two villages have a good contact and visit each other regularly mostly in the morning. Traditional indigenous or tribal knowledge of the Kokborok speaking people is also known as local knowledge, folk knowledge, people's knowledge, traditional wisdom or traditional science. The knowledge is passed from generation to generation, usually by word of mouth and cultural rituals, and has been the basis for agriculture, food preparation, health care, education, conservation and the wide range of other activities that sustain a society and its environment in many parts of the world for many centuries and is true in case of the Kokborok speaking people. In oral cultures of the Kokborok speaking people, much knowledge is owned and controlled by the community and by elderly both men and women. The elderly are very important and their memories and wisdom are vital to the survival of the whole group. Knowledge in oral cultures of the Kokborok speaking people is always transmitted by the elderly face to face, person to person, and usually in a group through storytelling, dance or ritual performance. Thus, the elderly are being part of a close society and strengthening the identity of the whole group and help in preserving the tradition of the community as a whole. In the dispute among the villagers or community the elderly are the first one to be consulted. However, this system is eroding as days passed by. In the interviews that was conducted, the elderly made it very clear that such erosion is due to modernization and side by side politics. The political structures have been responsible for the undermining of the traditional institutions.

However, now-a-days there are few cases of empty-nest syndrome found among the Kokborok speaking people. The case of Shri.Birmohan Debbarma, age 90+ years and Smt.Mayuri Debbarma, age 80+ years of chandithakur para is an example. They have five children (4 male and 1 female) but none of these children are with them now or within the village. All the four sons have been married to other villages. The only daughter is serving in the police department and is staying at Agartala and the parents are left to themselves. Such cases are on the rise and the society is not prepared to meet such situation. It may be because the society is closed and all the villagers are relatives, both of them get all kind of assistance as and when they require. But how long will that system work is a big question. If not today, but certainly tomorrow the tribal society of the Kokborok speaking people will have to address this issue very seriously.

The old age pension scheme is of great assistance to the elderly people of the Kokborok speaking people. Under the scheme of old age pension there are about 70 beneficiaries in Latia Chhera and 65 in Chikan Chhera. The monthly pension of Rs.600 (six hundred) is not enough but somehow for day to day expenses this amount is a great relief. There are many old age persons who are not able to get the scheme as one needs to qualify as below poverty line (BPL) and also needs to produce age proof certificate. In fact most of them are not aware of the date of birth and those who would qualify by age to get the scheme are depriving themselves. Also there are old age persons who are not categorized as BPL but deserve to get the old age pension scheme as there is no difference in their economic condition between them and the below poverty line.

REFERENCES

1. Interview with Sri Kajal Debbarma, Panchayat Secretary, Latia Chhere and Chikan Chhere Village Development Committee, Bishalgarh Sub-Division,West Tripura, dated.3rd December 2006.

2. Interview with Shri Birmohan Debbarma, (age 90+ years) and Smt Mayuri Debbarma, (age 80+ years) of chandithakur para(under Latia Chhere Village Development Committee) dated 3rd December 2006.

3. *The Times of India,* Kolkata, Nov.29 2006, p.9

4. Sukhendu Debbarma.' *Shifting Cultivation A Case Study among the Borok People of Tripura',* in the Proceedings of the North East India History Association, XIX Session, Kohima 1998, Shillong, 1999, pp. 199-205.

5. *Christianity in Tripura 1909-1990,* (Unpublished Ph.D Thesis), Submitted to the Department of History, North Eastern Hill University, Shillong, 2004.

4

Elderly Persons of Tripura: An Empirical Study

—Anjali Chakraborty

Introduction

Research in Gerontology (the study of aged and aging process),Geriatrics (the branch of medicine concerned with aging) and the sociological research have underlined the need for support services for the aged people, specially for the oldest, many of whom have outlined their savings and cannot pay for their own care. To enquire about the problems of the aged and to give some remedial suggestions is a good area of study for the Social Scientists of India. The constitution of India has provision (e.g. Article 41 and 42) for financial assistance to the aged persons. But this has drawn special attention from the government of India from 1995. Accordingly, initiatives have been taken for the social security of the old age persons. However, the problems still exist. Though India is a traditional society, absence of proper opportunities and suitable conditions are not there to utilize the elderly person's experiences and wisdom. Society has not yet provided with right conditions for them to live in a respectable way so that they may feel themselves useful to the society. Elderly people face many problems, which are not less significant than the problems faced in other stages of social life. In Tripura, there is no such study till date except some individual efforts. The Census Report of Tripura shows that in 1991, the aged people in the age group of 60 to 80 plus is 7.01 per cent of total population and in 2001, they are 7.27 per cent. The increasing number of older people in the present society of Tripura has definitely given rise to a lot of problems i.e. psychological, social, medical etc. Hence the study on the magnitude of the problems of elderly persons in Tripura is quite a need of the day.

Now a question arises, who the elderly persons are. The social scientists, specialized in the study of aging, refer to three groups of older adults:

a) the "young old" who belongs to the age group of 65 to 74 and who are active, vital and vigorous;

b) the "old old " belonging to the age group of 75 to 84 and (c) the "oldest old" belonging to the age group of 85 and above.

The latter two groups are more likely to be frail and infirm to manage the activities of daily life. In India, where the life expectancy is lower than those of the developed countries, three age groups may be read as 60-69, 70 to 79 and 80 plus. Besides the chronological age, there is the functional age i.e. how a person functions in a physical and social environment in comparison with others of same chronological age. Many persons are there whose functional age is below their actual age. They are much more active than their actual age-norm. Fact is that, most of the older persons, unless their health is poor, want to work and would continue it if they get employment. Even woman who did not work during the early years of adulthood when they were pre-occupied with the care of their children and homes, often return to work during middle age and find it a satisfactory substitute for the lost role of parenthood. The reasons of wanting to work are different for different people. But the opportunity for them to work with social prestige and participation is not sufficient to the increasing demands

However, old age is a period of decline. Decline comes mainly from physical side and also from mental side not due to a specific disease but to the natural aging process. This tends to aggravate in the absence of socio-economic insecurity. The social scientists, therefore, try to detect those points of insecurity of the aged persons and suggest some remedies to motivate the government and society.

An Empirical Study - Objectives

The present study aims to explore the problems faced by the elderly persons of Tripura, i.e., physical, psychological and especially in the socio-economic spheres of life. The study has been conducted through field investigation and the objectives of the study are

i. to assess the physical and mental state of the elderly persons of Tripura in the retired or post-service period i.e., whether they are suffering from any physical disease and mental disorder;

ii. to assess their social and financial contribution to the family as well as to the society;

iii. to gain a comparative assessment between two groups of elderly persons of different socio-economic status. And also on enquiry into their financial support, literacy status, and position in caste hierarchy, attitude of family members toward them and social acceptance and also mode of passing their time.

Methodology

Two different elderly persons' groups are selected for the purpose. Group I consists of the retired persons of Tripura Government residing in Agartala urban areas like Jogendranagar (Vidyasagar Chowmuhani), Dhaleswar, Arundhutinagar and Krishnanagar under the West Police Station. Forty-nine retired persons are selected as per convenience. They are school and college teachers, clerks, officer, secretary, director, journalist etc. For comparative analysis between economically independent and dependent groups, we have selected another group of old age people. Group II comprised of 50 women from an old age home namely "Apna Ghar" run by a NGO, *"Abalamban"* and it is situated at Barjala in Agartala. The Home is visited by the researcher. It is found that fifty women residents (48 widows, one unmarried, and one married woman) are totally dependent on the Home. No economic contribution is there from the side of the residents. They were mainly housewives; some of them worked as maid.

All respondents, 49 retired persons and 50 Home respondents, were asked both close and open-ended questions and also free dialogues were encouraged from them. They were asked about their physical and mental conditions and some socio-economic aspects related to their life. In addition to this primary information of field investigation, we have search for secondary sources of data like books, journals and Census Report of Tripura (1991 & 2001). The collected data have been examined and analyzed systematically for the purpose. However the result of this study on such a small group of retired persons and the group of inmates of the Home may not be generalized for whole Tripura.

Observations

The respondents were asked about their physical, psychological, economic and socio-cultural problems. The information given by the respondents along with our observation are noted here. It is observed that old age has direct impact on physical strength and stamina of the individuals. In the first group, out of the total 49 retired persons, 38 belongs to the age group of 60-69 and the rest 11 belongs to the age group of 70-80. Among them, 14 respondents are found physically fit; the rest 35 are suffering from some physical problems like osteoporosis, asthma, hypertension, indigestation, diabetics, eye-sight set back, nerve-oriented problem, arthritis, headache, weakness or lowered efficiency to work or partial loss of memory etc. The problem is acute only for few persons. Their activities are found restricted within a routine-life. In literacy status, they are graduates and post graduates. In the social hierarchy, they belong to the middle rank and status.

In the second group, many of the residents of *Apna Ghar* are found physically frail and infirm; suffering from the common physical problems said above. They belong to the age group of 60 to 74. Some cannot say their exact age. Some are found totally bed-ridden and dependent on others to move. They belong to low economic status and middle and low rank of Hindu caste-status. They are illiterate or literate in primary level. For exception, there is a case of a woman who belong to higher caste, middle class family having well established son and daughter. She has come here to enjoy her 'old age freedom'. The atmosphere of the Home is nice. Numbers of television sets are there for their recreation.

Psychological problems like senile dementia or alzheimer, depression or psychosis with cerebral arteriosclerosis are found totally absent among the pensioners— the first group, but partially present in the second group— the residents of *Apna Ghar*. The pensioners are suffering from some typical problems of old age, which are psychological in nature e.g. feeling of less useful in family and society; feeling of a pain as because their activities are restricted both in family and society; a subtle pain for the realization of truth that they are becoming physically weaker day by day and often some of them fail to reconcile the fact. They also suffer from some mental disturbances due to the conflict with younger ones or dependent, and their unsympathetic attitude towards them. However, they can reconcile the fact at last.

It is observed that they are trying to overcome their present physical problems and future probability of those problems by way of regulating their daily life. Most of them walk in every morning and evening, take lunch and dinner in time and do works daily e.g. bazar, gardening, reading newspaper, journals and various types of books; participating in religious rituals, listening the *Rabindra Sangeet* and other songs seeing television etc. some of them are writing poems, articles and practicing homeopathic medicine and astrology. Some are found very much inclined to religious activities not only within home but also at Ashrams, Missions etc. and thus in developing spiritual ideals. Some of them are found in self-employment e.g. establish small shops or business to help their sons to be established. The present data shows that both male and female pensioners are conscious and careful of their health. In the change of an held study we found that only few women participate in morning and evening walk, however most of them could not go for work as they are absorbed in family duties during such time.

Secondly, economic problems of the pensioners are found negligible. Being retired from Government service they are drawing pension according to their position and status in job. There is no case of the problems of procuring the pension money except one or two cases. Besides pension, there is the second line of income for many of them from different sources e.g. private tuitions, gardening and small business etc. In contrast, the residents of "Apna Ghar" are neither self-sufficient nor contributing the society. They worked in the early age of their life but have no such savings to maintain their own. There are no opportunities for them to participate in economic activities. They are engaged in works like washing (of their cloths) or other activities like stitching or knitting etc. and helping other inmates who are physically ill and sometimes engaged in personal prayer.

Thirdly, the socio-cultural aspect of the problem of old age is also significant. The retired parents have now enough time to give company to the family members and they pass their time by sometimes doing for the younger ones. They look after and cook for their grand children and also accompany them in going and coming from schools or other places. If they remain in distant place (e.g. Bombay, Rajasthan etc.) the mother often goes to live with the family of a married son or daughter who need them (They take care of them by physical labor and mental affection).The pensioner parents do not like to remain obliged to their children. In the present study, a pensioner mother about 70 years old, like to remain in self-dependent living in her own house in Arundhutinagar though her son and daughter living abroad care for her. She often visits them but never stay there for many days. As family is the first unit of society, women's contribution as mother or grandmother is important. The pensioner parents are found adjusting with their children. They have realized the truth that their experience of last fifty years may have little relevance to the problems of present generation. In the nuclear family environment, parents have adjusted themselves because they are self-sufficient and contribute something to the family. The sons living abroad come home to enjoy their company, as they love them. It is usually the case of middle class people who are self sufficient enough and the children are found very loyal to them, And also the dependents or less established sons or daughter care their parents more if the parents have bank balance or landed property.

On the contrary, the case is different for the residents of *Apna Ghar* who come from lower socio-economic strata. They are fully dependent for their physical, economic and medical care. It was revealed from their conversation that the emotional tie is somehow disturbed between parents and children, especially when the children perceive their parents as a burden. Therefore the conscious mothers and aunt want to live separated from their children to relieve them from economic pressure. At present, the mothers are living free-life staying at old age Home. They often go to visit their children or relatives and sometimes mothers are also visited by the sons and daughters. Not only financial but also complex mental relationship forced the residents of the Home to find out an alternative shelter.

No person of two groups blames the children except the fate. In the present state of life, the pensioners as well as the residents of Apana Ghar feel happy as the 'ghar' is their own. It is noted that the parents of both study groups, are found conscious of their personal freedom. In other words, they posses a sense of self-respect irrespective of their financial strength.

Suggestions

The above study on the problems of elderly persons in Tripura in two contrast groups of two socio-economic and educational background reveals that all the retired persons are self-sufficient not only in economic status but also in physical and psychological state of life. Even the oldest olds (70-79) are not dependent on their children. On the other hand the widows of *Apna Ghar* belonging to those same three age groups are dependent in all respects. Hence socio-economic background is an important factor to determine the role and status of elders in society. The study also reveals that not only the socio-economic factors, but also psychological factor is to be analyzed more. Because in both the groups, a loose emotional tie is obvious and usefulness of the person concerned is very much relevant for the status of old age in family and society.

The above study suggests some measures to minimize the problem of the old age:

i. Community Centre and Clinic should be there for assisting and counseling the older persons after retirement from government or private jobs, so that they can plan ahead for an active and useful life. Because those who continue to work have more normal brain functioning and are better adjusted than those who do not work. The old persons should prepare themselves to face changes realistically with mental flexibility and adaptability. Family members of the aged persons may be also given counseling about the ways of 'how to deal' with the aged.

ii. To provide them opportunities for work depending on experiences, efficiency and mental abilities rather than physical labor. Work should have some status value along with financial value so that they can think themselves useful to the society.

iii. There should be effective treatment for the older persons who are physically ill and mentally deranged. Government Institutions with free help are required for them.

iv. An arrangement of old age home is important. For various reasons, it is a cry of the day even in our tiny Tripura. Many people ask for a number of old age homes.

In fine, we are to keep in mind that "old age thus poses special problems, but it is by no means incompatible with meaning and self fulfillment (Coleman).

REFERENCES

1. Census Report, Tripura (1991, 2001).
2. Rao, C.N. Sarkar, (2001). *Sociology: Primary Principles*. Manak Publication Pvt. Ltd.
3. Elezabath Hurlock, (1959). *Developmental Psychology*. McGrow Hill.
4. Papalia, Sally Wendks, Olds, Feldman,(1960). *Human Development*.

5

Prevalence of Coronary Heart Disease (CHD) and Congestive Heart Failure (CHF) Among Elderly in Tripura – Lessons and Directions

—Atanu Ghosh and Beenapani Doley

Introduction

Ageing of the population is a significant product of epidemiological transition from communicable diseases to chronic degenerative diseases. In India the proportion of older persons has risen from 4.9 per cent in 1901 to 5.5 per cent in 1951, 7.7 per cent in 2001 and will be 12 per cent in 2020.[1] Epidemiological transition, with increasing life expectancy (currently it is 64 yrs in the country) and[2] demographic shifts in age profile is accelerating the CHD epidemic in India. CHD prevalence in Indian urban population increased from 3.5per cent in 1960 to 9.5per cent in 1990.[3] There is neither a population based nor a hospital based prevalence study of CHD in Tripura. Currently Echocardiography unit of G B Hospital Agartala has undertaken a retrospective10 year study of prevalence of Heart diseases on the basis of analysis of Echocardiography studies made from 1995 to 2006 (No. of patients 9195). The present paper is a sub group analysis of impact of CHD and CHF in the elderly.

Aim

To study the profile of CHD and CHF in elderly population of Tripura.

Design

A retrospective study.

Materials and methods

Echocardiography is the hallmark for diagnosis of Coronary Heart Disease and Congestive Heart Failure. It is non invasive and easy to perform and is in practice in G B Hospital, Agartala since 1992. More than 11,000 studies have been made so far in the Echo Laboratory. A prevalence study is currently being carried out on the basis of records available in the Laboratory Analysis for a period of 5 (five) years from 1.1.2002 to 30.9.2006 covering a sample size of 6002 have been completed.

We studied 500 and 176 consecutive reports of echo cardiographically diagnosed cases of CHD and CHF respectively from 1.1.2005 to 30.9.2006 at G B Hospital. Inclusive criteria of Regional Wall Motion abnormality and/or loss of wall thickness in systole for CHD and LV dimension of >55 mm and EF below 40per cent for CHF are made.

Results

On going study covering so far a period of 5 years

from 1.1.2002 to 30.9.2006 reveal a total of 6002 studies made in echocardiography Unit for diagnosis of heart diseases in patients whose signs and symptoms point to a possibility of heart disease. The prevalence noted are CHD (n 1346) 22.4 per cent, Rheumatic Heart Disease (RHD) (n 472) 7.8 per cent, Cardiomyopathy (n 606) 10.3 per cent, Congenital Heart Disease (n 348) 5.7per cent. Other cardiac diseases like Diastolic LV dysfunction, Hypertensive LVH, Mitral Valve Prolapse, Pericardial diseases, Atherosclerotic Valve diseases (in order of frequency) together accounted for (n 1854) 30.9per cent. The rest (n 1376) 22.9 per cent (Table 1) made up of normal studies. They do not exclude CHD, but is excluded from study because of absence of any criterion as described earlier.

Table 1
Heart Disease prevalence in G B Hospital, Agartala

Disease	*No. of cases*	*Per cent*
CHD	1346	22.4
Rheumatic Ht Ds	472	7.8
Cardiomyopathy	606	10.3
Congenital Ht Ds	348	5.7
Other forms of Heart Ds	1854	30.9
Normal Study	1376	22.9
Total	6002	100

Highest prevalence of CHD is seen in age group 61 and above (n 478) 35.7per cent and lowest below 40 years (n 87) 6.4per cent. (Table 2).

Table 2.
Age group analysis of CHD patients in G B Hospital, Agartala.

Age Group in years	*No. of CHD patients*	*Per cent*
<40	87	6.4
41-50	323	23.9
51-60	458	34.0
61 & above	478	35.7
Total	1346	100

Below normal EF (<50per cent) is noticed in (n 915) 67.9 per cent CHD cases for all age group, the rest have normal EF.

Sub-group analysis (500 consecutive CHD cases) revealed a prevalence of (n 352) 69.7per cent CHD among elderly (>50yrs) age group, the oldest being 90 years old. The rest (30.3per cent) belong to young and adult (<50 yrs) age groups, the youngest being 20 years old. The male female ratio of elderly CHD is 3:1. 49.6 per cent elderly Male patients have below normal EF, whereas it is more (57.9 per cent) in case of elderly female (Table 3).

Table 3
EF Profile of Elderly Patients

Sex of Patient	*EF<50per cent*	*EF>50 per cent*	*Total*
Male	131	133	264
Female	51	37	88
Total	180	172	352

More than half (51.5per cent) of all elderly CHD group exhibited below normal EF (<50 per cent).Below normal EF(<50 per cent) observed in age group 50-60 is 46.3 per cent, 60.8 per cent in age group 61-70 and 51.5 per cent in 71 and above age group.Table 4.

Table 4

Elderly and low EF relationship

Age of Patient	EF<50 per cent	EF>50 per cent	Total
50-60	90	104	194
61-70	56	36	92
71& above	34	32	66
Total	180	172	352

The CHD patients from Urban areas have a marginal edge over patients from Rural areas (57 per cent against 43 per cent), whereas CHF patients from Rural areas make up majority of 56 per cent over Urban CHF patients. Because of the distance a considerable number of rural CHD patients may die before reaching the base hospital at Agartala. Apart from poor nutritional status of rural group, lack of appropriate treatment may contribute to surge of CHF patients in rural community.

Sub group analysis for CHF revealed a prevalence of 64.7per cent among elderly group with EF below 40 per cent together with LV dilatation.

Thus it can be concluded that burden of CHD and CHF in Tripura lie heavily against the elderly.

Hospital Based CHD prevalence studies in India

CHD cases as proportion of total cardiac admissions/ IPD attendance varied from 10-25per cent, depending on the location of the hospital. The reported prevalence are 11per cent in Delhi, 22 per cent in Amritsar, 15 per cent in Bombay, 13 per cent in Madras, 10 per cent in Lucknow, 11 per cent in Mysore and 24 per cent in Chandigarh.[4] Our findings (22 per cent) are comparable to those of Amritsar and Chandigarh. It is a very shocking revelation that a place like Agartala having no industrial economic activity can have such a high prevalence of CHD. Centers which reported high CHD prevalence like Chandigarh, Amritsar and our present study have a common feature of high population of displaced persons from West Punjab and East Bengal. There is no data available on the subject from Eastern and North-Eastern states.

Population Based Cross-sectional Epidemiological Surveys

Initial epidemiological studies were performed in late 1950s in Agra (Mathur, 1960) and Delhi (Padmavati 1962)[5] in the urban population the prevalence increased from 1.05 per cent (Agra 1962) to 6.60 per cent (Chandigarh 1968) to 9.67 per cent (Delhi 1990) and 12.65 per cent (Trivandrum 1995) in rural population the prevalence increased from 2.06 per cent (Haryana 1974) to 7.43 per cent (Kerala 1993).[6]

Mortality statistics

In 1998 the annual death rate for India was 840/100,000 population. Cardiovascular diseases contribute to 27 per cent of these deaths and its crude mortality rate was 227/100,000. Mortality rate in different Indian states vary from 75-100 in sub Himalayan states of Nagaland, Meghalaya, Sikkim and Himachal Pradesh to a high of 360-430 in Andhra Pradesh, Tamil Nadu, Punjab and Goa.[7]

In 2002 death due to Cardiovascular diseases of 2.78 million took place in India and CHD alone caused 1.51 million deaths followed by deaths due to cerebrvascular strokes, Hypertensive diseases, Rheumatic Heart Disease (RHD).[8]

Salient features of CHD and CHF in Elderly in Tripura:

1. High prevalence of CHD (22.4 per cent) in Tripura in all age group. This is comparable to hospital based studies of Amritsar and Chandigarh. All the three centers have a high population of displaced persons.
2. Highest prevalence (35.7 per cent) of CHD is seen in age group 61 and above.
3. Male/Female ratio of elderly CHD is 3:1.
4. Elderly female CHD patients tend to have lower EF than male, consequently they have poorer prognostic outcome.
5. Lowest level of EF is seen in age group 61-70 years, which is associated with low Quality Of Life (QOL) and frequent hospitalizations.
6. 64.7 per cent of all cases of CHF belong to elderly age group.
7. The urban/rural distribution of CHD is 57 per cent against 43 per cent. Whereas, CHF is more prevalent in rural areas which is 56 per cent against 44 per cent in urban areas.

Thus the burden of CHD and CHF is heavily placed against elderly age group in Tripura and they affect adversely their quality of life.

High prevalence of CHD in elderly and socioeconomic factors

1. Life expectancy in India continues to grow since independence. This is the result of decline in deaths in infancy, childhood, and adolescence due to improvement in public health. Improved socioeconomic indicators like per capita income and female literacy contributed to the decline in infectious and nutritional deficiency disorders. The increasing longevity provides longer periods of exposure to the risk factors of CHD, resulting in greater possibility of CHD in elderly.
2. The second contributing factor for the surge in CHD in elderly is the growth of population. In India, for example, the population is expected to rise from 683.2 million in 1981 to somewhere between 1253.8 and 1480.5 million in 2021. Simultaneously, the proportion of adults aged 35 years or above will rise from 28.4 per cent of the population to 42.4 per cent.[9]
3. A third contributor is the adverse life style changes accompanying industrialization and urbanization. Increase in the body weight, high blood pressure, diabetes, raised cholesterol levels and increasing use of tobacco, all contribute to higher prevalence of CHD in elderly.

Thrifty Gene

The "thrifty gene" hypothesis has been postulated to be a factor in promoting selected survival, over generations, of persons who encountered an adverse environment of limited nutritional resources. It has been postulated that populations subjected to food scarcity have undergone selection of a gene which increases the efficiency of fat storage through an over secretion of insulin in response to meal. While this favors survival in a situation of scarcity, a current excess of calorie intake may lead to obesity, hyperinsulinemia, diabetes and atherosclerosis.[10]

Maternal-fetal exposure as a cause of mid life CHD.

The "fetal origin hypothesis" states that adverse intra uterine influences like poor maternal nutrition lead to impaired fetal growth resulting in low birth weight, short birth length, and a small head circumference. As the child grows, they tend to have an increased risk of glucose intolerance, hypertension and dyslipidemia in later life.[11]

How to reverse CHD epidemic

Lessons from developed countries

During the last 30 years in the USA, the CHD mortality rate has decreased for all age groups. Between 1968 and 1978, the CHD mortality rate decreased by 28 per cent for persons aged 65 to 74 and by 19 per cent for those aged 75 to 84.[12] Furthermore, persons appear to be reaching old age with less severe atherosclerotic disease.

Factors contributing to the decreased severity of atherosclerosis and CHD mortality rate include reductions in cholesterol levels and smoking and diabetes prevalence as well as better control of hypertension.

Risk Factors of CHD in elderly

Risk factors for CHD in elderly men and women include cigarette smoking, systolic and/or diastolic hypertension, increased pulse pressure, increased serum total and low-density lipoprotein(LDL) cholesterol level, decreased serum high-density lipoprotein(HDL) cholesterol level, diabetes mellitus, obesity, physical inactivity, advancing age, increased coronary intimal-medial thickness, and hyperhomocyctenimia. Hypertriglyceridemia is a risk factor for women.

Directions for arresting CHD epidemic in Tripura

Management of Modifiable Risk Factors

Modifiable risk factors for CHD should be controlled. Cessation of cigarette smoking, treatment of hypertension and hyperlipidemia, maintenance of a normal body weight, and regular physical activity lower the risk of CHD and new coronary events. A diet low in saturated fat and cholesterol is recommended. For obese persons, regular aerobic exercise and a healthy diet are recommended. Moderate exercise programme suitable for the elderly include walking, climbing stairs, swimming and bicycling.

Because the prevalence of CHD is higher in the elderly than in younger persons, risk factor modifications cause a greater reduction in the absolute number of coronary events in the elderly.

Socioeconomic Approach

Nutritional Care from fetus to adolescence can prevent mid life CHD in India to a great extent as causal relationship of under nutrition and CHD is established in developing countries. The directions include:

1. Improvement of Maternal and Child Health (MCH) services.
2. Female literacy.
3. Improvement of Public Distribution Services (PDS).
4. Balance in procurement price of food grain and minimum support price with a view to reduce price of food grain.
5. Mid Day Meals in Schools.

Hospital Services

1. The number of CCU and ICU beds in Tripura is far below the required need. It is essential to increase their strength soon.
2. There should be special OPD services for senior citizens in each specialty hospital.
3. There should be change of strategy from Surgery and Angioplasty to Poly pill pharmacy. The surgery and Angioplasty gives relief from Angina Pain but does not improve mortality. More over the procedures are very expensive and beyond the reach of 99 per cent of our population.[13]
4. As CHD is not curable, attention should be given on detection, maintenance of registry, training of paramedics and palliative management.
5. Study of Geriatrics as a separate discipline in Medical College.

Secondary Prevention

Those with diagnosed CHD and or Diabetes/

Hypertension, should be treated with Aspirin, ACE Inhibitors, Statin (Poly Pill Pharmacy) in adequate doses.

Acknowledgement

Authors are grateful to Principal, AGMC and M.S., G B Hospital, Agartala for the use of hospital records.

REFERENCES

1. Vinode Kumar. *Geriatric Medicine.* API text Book of Medicine. Shah S N (API Mumbai 2003): 1459-1462.
2. Yeolkar M.E., *Elderly in India – Needs & Issues.* JAPI. 2005; 53:843-844.
3. Gupta R, Meta-analysis of Coronary Heart Disease Prevalence in India. *Indian Heart Journal* 1996; 48:241-245.
4. Sapru R P. An overview of Cardiovascular Diseases in India. Editor Wasir HS. *Preventive Cardiology.* New Delhi, Vikas Publishing House; 1991:69-86.
5. Gupta R, Gupta VP. Meta analysis of Coronary Heart Disease in India.*IHJ* 1996; 48: 241-245.
6. *The World Health Report 2002;* Geneva: WHO; 2002.
7. *The World Health Report 2004*; Geneva: WHO; 2004.
8. Reddy KS. Cardiovascular Disease in India; *World Health Statement 1993*; 46: 101-107.
9. Pearson TA. *Global Perspective of Cardiovascular Diseases. Evidence Based Cardiovascular Medicine.* 1997; 1: 4-5.
10. K Srinath Reddy. *Global Perspective of Cardiovascular Diseases. Evidence Based Cardiology. 1998;* 1; 147-164.
11. *The Merck Manual of Geriatrics,* Ch. 88; Coronary Artery Disease.
12. Enas A. Enas. Arresting and reversing the epidemic of CAD in India. *Current perspective in Cardiology.* Editor Anil Kumar. 52 CSI, Chtennai. 2000; 109-128.

6

Study of the Health Aspect of Elderly at Sandhyanir-Bridhya Ashram at Gandhi Gram, Tripura West

—Arun Ghosh

Background

Health status of senior citizens needs medical study. The discussion turned from old age pensions and railway concessions to health related advancements and genetic factors in dementia. In India elderly especially urban advocates the policy not only social welfare department but the planning commission. Now every department of the government is involved with the special needs and requirements of the elderly. The impetus to elderly concerns in India can be traced in to three main developments- first evolution of civil society and a mature democracy expanding social commitment of the state like Tripura. Secondly demographic transition of the state and 3rd factor is related to the growth of activism and advocacy by groups of elderly, non government organization, and academicians. Consequently a national policy for older persons has finally been formulated enshrining the states commitment towards its aging population.

Introduction

In 1988 it was estimated 159 million persons aged 65 in developing countries compared to 140 million in developed countries. This short study was carried out at "Sandhynir" (Bridaa Ashram) located at Gandhigram 10 km away from the Agartala city which was established in 2001 and registered under Society Act 2004. This cross- sectional study among elderly people is based on "cluster sampling technique" in particular section who are staying together for long time.

Aims and Objectives

1. To determine the pattern of treatment seeking, disability, psychological distress, socioeconomic variables in elderly group.
2. To find out the psychological well-being for better understanding of the relation between perceived health, chronic illness and disabling condition.
3. To study the pattern of distribution by rural urban location, age, sex of elderly.
4. To asses the magnitude of medical problems/ illness/ disease status.

Material and Methods

This study has been carried out among the elderly inmates of "Sandhyanir" at Gandhigram in the year 2006. Thirty elderly persons are taken in to account of that Bridya-ashram with the help of Society comprises 25 members from all section of the society. The Ashram is free of noise, pollution and with attractive natural beauty. The Society is not taking help from Government.

For assessment of disability - (The standardized rapidly disability rating scale) consisting of 18 items in 2 group - Part –A;- deals with ADL-(assessment of daily living) focused on, walking, bathing, dressing, toileting, grooming, adaptive tasks and eating. Part-2 B; - assessed by communication, hearing, vision, diet, locomotion, mental efficiency,

Again dividing the total subjects in different categories to asses the disability- as shown in the table: a) minimal disability – do not require any assistance or care b) Moderately disabled - require some medication c) Severe group need hospitalization.

Psychological distress also assessed by different questionnaires

The subjects were interviewed by me and recorded their socio-demographic data, the illness/disease status as per protocol. The interviewees were also asked to display the container of all medication and to show the all reports they possessed. Subsequently the symtomatology was noted and general physical examination was carried out. Based on reported illness, clinical features, medical records, and the medication they had with them. A provisional clinical diagnosis was made according to international classification of diseases. Information on treatment seeking behavior, any surgical operation, hospital admission and socio demographic variables used were age, sex, martial status, occupation and source of income(classified low income group). Proxy interviews of the society member Sri. P. Roybarman, Sr. advocate are also taken in this regard.

Result- out of 30 subjects, all are above 60 years of age. Table-1 shows 63.33 per cent are female and 36.67 per cent are male respectively. All are unmarried with low economic status. Table-2 shows the rural and urban distributions are 86.60 per cent and 13.33 per cent respectively. Table-3 the degree of disability among 30 subjects is minimal 23.33 per cent, moderate 70.0 per cent and severe 6.66 per cent respectively. Among the total subjects 93.33 per cent are having no psychological distress only 6.66 per cent are having physical psychological distress (table-4). The distribution of age (table-5) are having 60-65 years (60 per cent), 66-70 yrs (23.33 per cent), 71-75 yrs (10 per cent), and 76-80 (6.67 per cent) respectively. Table-6 showing the magnitude of medical problems in health aspects among the cluster group, visual impairment 73.33 per cent, hearing declination 63.33 per cent, hypertension 53.33 per cent insomnia 46.67 per cent respiratory tract 43.33 per cent heartburn 23.33 per cent operation (cataract) 10 per cent, kyphosis 6.67 per cent respectively.

Discussion of results

Marital status has the greatest impact on living arrangements of the elderly population. In developing countries the proportion of person aged 65 years and above who live alone ranges from 10 per cent (Japan) to 90 per cent (Sweden). This proportion is smaller in India because both married and widowed older persons commonly live with their children and grand children. (Joshi, Sengupta, Health Issue 2006) In India, the nation wide survey conducted by National Sample Survey Organization (NSSO 1991) reported that the elderly living alone was 6 and 8 per cent respectively for the urban and rural area. In this selective study all subjects are unmarried

70 per cent are from urban and 34 per cent are from rural (NSSO-1991), IJE 2003 91 per cent from urban but in this study rural 86.67 per cent which is not similar with others.

In developing country like India there are more old men than women (NSSO) but here it is reverse.

This study shows 60 per cent elderly belongs to 60 – 65 years of age which is close with NSSO study. Sunder et.al ., also shows that 65 years group is common having 89.6 per cent, IJE 94.5 per cent in this regard.

About disability IJE 2003 study shows out of their total study 22 per cent of subjects had minimal disability 48.5 per cent had moderate disability and 17 per cent from severe disability. But in this cluster study minimal 23.33 per cent, moderate 70 per cent severe 6.6 per cent similar with the study of Joshi, et al PGI Chandigarh.

Comparative evaluation of magnitude of medical health problems with other workers in India.

Problems	per cent	per cent	per cent	per cent Tripura
Visual impairment	61 (IJE-2003,Joshi et al, Chandigarh	88 impairment (Maduari-TN venkoba Rao –1990)	13.6 Kishore &garg IJE *65percent (Haryana sundar et al)	65 (persent study)
Hearing impairment	20 (IJE-2003)	8 (Madurai-TN)	18.3 (Haryana)	63.33 (persent
Hypertension	5.2 (kishore & Garg)	16.5 (Garg)	17 (Madurai)	53.33 (persent study)

Insomonia	5 (IJE)	14 (Madurai TN)	-	46.67
Respiratory tract infection(cough, breathing difficulty)	52 (IJE)	58 (Rohtak sundr et al)	-	43.33 (persent study)
Heart burn	10 (Madurai -TN)	9.9 (Rrohtak)	-	23.33
Cataract	30 (Garg & Kishore)	24 Garg	-	6.66 (persent) study)
Operation	27 (IJE)		-	10 (persent study)
Locomotor system (Kyphosis)	14 IJE Garg	40 (Madurai-TN	-	6.67 (persent study)

Analysis

In contrast to other findings this study have reported that condition like visual impairment,hearing impairment, hypertension ,respiratory tract infection ,heart burn etc were associated with low label of disability. Here the subjects are not seeking any treatment due to regular treatment and check up by a physician. They do not have depression, feeling of loneliness because they stay together and getting good care and supervision.

Limitation of the study

The proxy rating is true and based on reality. As it is for particular section does not reflect the state. It is important because it is able to show the various factors that are related to functional status and psychological well being of elderly people in this state.

Future Direction

In order to improve the health status of the elderly population, it is important to carry out more studies in different areas to identify various factors that are related to psychological distress and disability, which should lead to efforts to develop effective programmes in disease prevention.

Failure

This study could not observe the nutritional status among the elderly subjects i.e. intake of fruits, leafy green vegetables, and milk and other diet related to nutrition etc., No wonder most of our elderly population reports nutritional problem. The infection rate remains high among the poor nutrition people.

This survey could not elicit other medical problems like malignancy, cardiovascular disease (CVD), TB, emotional and other organic problem.

Conclusion

There is an assumption that disease and deterioration of ill health are inevitably associated with chronological ageing. Some elderly persons are sick while others maintain health status even into advanced age. The main risk factors are loss of fortune, fall in self esteem, sense of helplessness, poor education, substandard health, social and gender discrimination, financial debt and status etc.

Therefore the elderly receive adequate state and social support to live an active and social productive life. At the minimum require comprehensive health care directed to elderly in particularly equipping our PHC in geriatric care.

Fortunately our cultural ethos gives a special place to the elderly as wise people and counselors of society. Both geriatric support and social engineering aimed at improving the competence of the elderly and ensuring their active participation in society should be considered together in evolving any policy on aging care. The experience and wisdom of old age is treasure for any society, its gainful utilization would be beneficial for both elderly as well as the younger generation.

Acknowledgement

I express my heartful gratitude to the dwellers of sandhyanir who have shown their cooperation in all respect and the society who have permitted me to take this study. In addition I express my sincere and special thanks to Sr. Advocate P. Roybarman for his lawful cooperation.

REFERENCES

1. K. Kinsella and C.M. Taebur, *An Aging World-US Government* Washington DC 1992, UNDP 1990.
2. J.S. Seigel, Demographic aspects of health of the elderly to the year 2000 and beyond, *World Health 1982*.
3. NSSO, "Socioeconomic profile of aged persons", *Sarvekshana*, 15(1-2), 1991.
4. A.Venkaba Rao, *Health Care of Rural Age*, ICMR, New Delhi, 1990.
5. *International Journal of Epedemiology*, 2003, pp. 32978-987.

7

Geriatric Medical Services in Tripura – A Future Guideline

—Sushanta Kumar Sen

Introduction

Ageing is a universal process. It is a normal inevitable biological phenomenon. The word 'Geriatrics' has been derived from Greek 'geras' means 'old age' and 'iatrikos' means 'healing'. It is the branch of medical science that deals with the old age and its diseases. This branch of medical science did not develop much in the past, as the per centage of geriatric population was very less in the society. Now, due to advancement of medical science in last few decades mortality rate and birth rate have been reduced. Life expectancy at birth has increased. This group of the society has become a special component to be taken care of.

Demographic picture

Demographic structure of every country is changing gradually with large number of old people in the society. In India, due to advancement of medical science, successful implementation of different national health programs and increase in health consciousness among people, death rate and birth rate is reduced significantly. Life expectancy at birth has now been increased to 67.04 years for male and 69.1 years for female.

It was estimated that in India, 3.5 per cent and 6.8 per cent of the population were above 65 years of age in 1981 and 1991 respectively. At present approximately 7.5 crores people in India belong to geriatric age group. This number would become 17.7 crores and 24.3 crores in 2011 and 2051 respectively.

In Tripura, approximately, 1, 27,489 that is 4.6 per cent of total population were above 65 years in 1991 census. Life expectancy at birth in Tripura have been estimated as 54.1 years, 57.6 years and 64 years for male and 57.7 years, 57.1 years and 64 years for female in 1981, 1991 and 2001 Census respectively.

These data clearly show that geriatric population should be considered as a special group and a new discipline named **«Geriatric Medicine»** should be introduced in our healthcare delivery system both in public and private sector.

Health problems of the geriatric population can be classified as follows:

A. Problems solely due to aging process - Senile Cataract, Glaucoma, Nerve Deafness, Body changes affecting mobility, Emphysema, failure of special senses and changes in mental out look.

B. Problem associated with long term illness - Chronic diseases like degenerative diseases of heart and blood vessels; Cancer of the Prostate Gland; accidental fracture Neck of Femur due to trivial injuries; Diabetes; diseases of loco motor system like Fibrositis, Myositis,

Neuritis, Gout, Rheumatoid Arthritis, Osteoarthritis and Spondylitis; Respiratory diseases like Chronic Bronchitis, Asthma, Emphysema etc.; diseases of Genitourinary system like enlargement of Prostate, dysuria, nocturia, increased frequency and urgency of micturition are very common problems in geriatric age group.

C. Psychological problems - People of geriatric age group suffer from impaired memory, rigidity of outlook and dislike for changes.

It has to be mentioned that the elderly health conditions and management thereof is largely dependent on the socioeconomic and family situations. Due to multiple factors, people of this age group suffer from maladjustment in the society and family. People of this age group are non-working and are often financially dependant. They have to depend financially on their family for livelihood and medical care, as in our country role of State for taking care of their wellbeing is negligible. Even there are very few insurance schemes in this regard. The sense of being ignored by the family and being a financial burden to the society as well as on the family makes them suffer from melancholy and depression. This problem is gradually increasing in the age of **'Nuclear Family'** and the rapidly growing **'Consumer Society'**.

Initiatives to be started

Introducing the facilities for the aged in the out patient department (OPD) of the state level hospitals, these may be extended to in patient department (IPD) and other public and private hospitals gradually. In the long term geriatric wards and then geriatric hospitals may be planned.

Immediate Short Term measures to be taken up in G.B. Pant Hospital and IGM Hospital.

A. Clinical Services in OPD

Single Window Services To avoid hustles there should be provision for many services from a single center.

Service Counter– There should be single counter for registration and cash collection.

Geriatric Clinic–A separate Geriatric Clinic may be introduced in GBP Hospital and IGM Hospital. There should be adequate waiting space with seating arrangement in front of the clinic. Subsequent specialist consultation may be operated from this clinic. Every geriatric patient may be issued a Health Card with his/her photograph on first visit in the Geriatric Clinic. His/her physical conditions should be entered in detail. Some routine tests should be done and entered in the Card. This Card would be used on successive visits.

iii. Dispensing -There should be separate counter for geriatric patients in the Dispensary.

iv. Diagnostic services

a. *Pathology* - A separate Collection Center with enough seating arrangement should be provided on the ground floor for collection of samples.

Screening for early detection of malignancies

These patients may be screened routinely for early detection of malignancies common in this age group.

These are: Exfoliative Cytology for early detection of Cancer of Cervix, Faecal Occult Blood Test to detect Colo-rectal Carcinoma (positive cases may be advised for Sigmoidoscopy, Barium Enema and Biopsy), tests for H.Pylori as incidences of Carcinoma of Stomach is more among the positive cases of H. Pylori, Nasopharyngeal Swab Test for early detection of Carcinoma of Larynx, Hepatitis Surface Antigen Test (Hb_sAg) as Hb_sAg positive cases are susceptible for Carcinoma of Liver (Hepatoma).

b. ***Radio diagnosis*** – These patients should get priority for all Radiological tests to be done on the same day to avoid a second visit for this purpose.

c. ***Special Tests***– Early appointment to be given for special tests like Sonography, Echocardiography etc.

v. ***Surgical Intervention***– Minor Surgical interventions may be done on the first visit and for major surgical intervention appointment should be given early.

B. Clinical Services in IPD

In every Ward some beds may be earmarked for the geriatric patients. If bed is not available, accommodation may be made on the floor providing a mattress. Diagnostic services should be initiated immediately after admission.

C. ***Ancillary Services***– There should be a group of four workers/ volunteers for ambulation of these patients within the hospital. NGOs may take part in this sector.

II. Measures in the long term

i. **Separate Geriatric Wards** - Separate Geriatric

Multidisciplinary Wards one for male and other for female may be constructed in G.B. and IGM Hospital.

ii. ***Home Care Services*** – This service can be rendered at the patient's house. These include nursing, feeding and psychiatric counseling etc. to the debilitating patients. NGOs/ Nursing Associations/ Social Welfare Organizations may work in this area.

iii. ***Geriatric Services at District Hospitals*** – Geriatric Services should be introduced at District Hospitals in the same model as done in State Hospitals at first phase.

iv. ***Health Insurance Scheme*** – Health Insurance Scheme may be introduced with co-payment from the employer and employee.

A 100 bedded Geriatric Hospital may be constructed at Agartala both in public and private sector.

8

Old age Traumas and Attempts for its Alleviation in Tripura

—D. Ganchaudhuri

The problems of old age are complex and familial, eternal and universal. These problems vary from country to country, culture to culture and family to family. Tripura stands no exception. There is no permanent solution to these inevitable problems. One has to face them with courage, imagination and sympathy. What follows is a brief study relating to ageing and Governmental and non-governmental programmes which provide services to the elderly people of Tripura.

'Old-age' has no common and general yardstick. In the U.S.A. it is 65+ but in Korea it is 45+. The United Nations Organisation has declared 60+ as the last frontier of our lives. Professors of Tripura University retire at the age of 65 years; in Colleges the age of superannuation is 60 but other Government employees in Tripura retire from their service at the age of 58. In gerontology, ageing means the progressive changes that take place in a cell, a tissue, an organ system, a total organism or a group of organisms with the passage of time. All living things change with time in both structure and function and the changes that follow a general trend constitute ageing. Ageing is unavoidable part of the developmental sequence of the entire life span. Beginning with conception, this developmental sequence includes prenatal growth and development, birth, infancy, childhood, adolescence, maturity and senescence. Ageing is a natural and normal part of this total process.

Methodology

In this empirical study of old-age-related problems and programmes, an attempt has been made to review the existing and ever growing literature on gerontology. Attention is given more to the local issues than to the controversial definition and other problems of old age. Here the focus is on the attempts of a few real-world people to solve some real-world problems.

Bewilderment

When the smoke and dust of the great partition (1947) had not yet been settled, Tripura faced ethnic problem. Throughout the second half of the twentieth century, Tripura had to struggle against heavy odds. Thus one problem after another appeared in turn. Now, the familial problem of old age has come to the surface. In a country where the upward mobility has become the powerful trend, and where advancement of the children has been the mission and vision of the grand-parents and parents, a deep sigh of the aged people has been suddenly heard. Those who have nursed and fed the children with love and labour, find the grown-ups parting, living in new place of habitation, running after their own career and often neglecting the norms of family solidarity. Many of these old people worked hard and sacrificed their yesterday for the child's tomorrow. In return, the 'lucky' ones get what they expect in old age. But for many others a secured life eludes them. It implies a sad inconsistency between the commandments of the Indian civilization (Manu, 4/21) and the imperatives of their experience. The balance of power is being shifted on the side of new locality with nuclear family. With old age comes loss of prestige, position, power and purse and loss of physical strength, social contacts and activities.

Intergenerational gap

An enquiry into today's intergenerational gap among grandparents, parents and children and also into inter regional 'gap' may be useful. Tripura consists of hills and valleys, many villages and a few towns. The socio-economic situation between rural life and city-life varies. In the country side, life mostly follows the same old patterns. Agriculture, animal husbandry, cottage industry etc. constitute the main economic base. Joint family, nuclear family, patrilocality and family solidarity are to be found even today in the rural areas. Agartala, the capital city, has a different picture. Trade and commerce, bureaucratic jobs, industry, nuclear family, neolocality, enormous agglomerations of houses and buildings arranged in rows of roads and very high cost of land dotted with academies and administrative offices indicate the life of Agartala. Agartala was not what it is now. The city is being increasingly filled with a roar of traffic from morning till night. Agartala may be taken as the ideal example to form an idea of the town life of Tripura.

It follows that intergenerational 'gap' among grandparents, parents and children are minimum in the countryside, and maximum in the city of Agartala. Tripura's merger with the Indian Union in 1949 has given great impetus to education, modernization and bureaucratic jobs. This impetus too has widened the gap between the persons born long before 1949 and those born after 1949. In the countryside it is a common scene to see grandparents, parents, children, uncles, aunts, cousins and kins living in the same village, building homes around a common courtyard, worshipping the village-deities and participating the festivals. Household chores are divided along the traditional lines. Husband and wife occasionally go away leaving the children to the care of the grandparents. The situation is, however, different in Agartala; here many women also work as office clerks, teachers, waitresses, typists etc. The family depends on her income, and money makes her independent. She handles the family finances and wields considerable influence in the family. The urban nuclear family is a place where she can exercise her authority, where she can find needs and comforts well attended. The constraints of joint family are absent here. So a new wife's first intention is to break her husband's attachment to his parents and brothers and then to settle in and around Agartala. The new couple's next attempt is to stabilize their financial condition and then face the responsibilities of parenthood.

No wonder that most of the old age homes have been set up in and around Agartala. In a sense, it is the case of a life between settled living and sophisticated living. The norms of sophisticated living in urban setting seem to victimize the elderly people.

Informal Support

In the past, distress caused by accident, calamity or old age was looked upon as a personal, familial problem. It was the responsibility of the members of the family, relatives and kins to come with aid and advice.

Britain: Beveridge Report

In modern times, Britain has taken the lead in extending political democracy to the economic and social spheres. The Beveridge Report (1942) was a landmark in this respect. It involved governmental responsibilities for improving the quality of life of the citizens. Under this scheme social security endeavours to maintain a minimum standard of living when old age robs on individual of normal sources of livelihood.

Indian Scriptures and Acts

The ancient Indian saints and law-givers had the wisdom to it an obligatory duty on the part of the children. The *Taittoriya Upanishad* (1.11.1-4), the *Manusmriti* (4.21), the *Gita* (3.13) etc. have laid down clear directions. Recently the Hindu Adoptions and Maintenance Act, 1956 and the Code of Criminal Procedure, 1973 made it a legal obligation. Not only that, the Government of India and the provincial governments have opened social welfare departments and have been providing financial assistance worth crores of rupees annually. The Senior Citizens' (Maintenance, Protection and Welfare) Bill 2006 introduced in the Parliament of India by Sushma Swaraj is another step in the right direction.

Tripura Government's Pioneering Attempt

It is interesting to note that the Government of

Tripura did a pioneering job in establishing the first old age home in Tripura in 1961. The Government of Tripura can claim credit for framing a model code in 1972. This code, Prospectus of Infirmary, 1972, laid down specific rules and regulations, procedures and provisions for the supervisors and infirms. It may serve as a model for the voluntary agencies also.

Education Department of the Government of Tripura has set up the State Infirmary at Narsingarh on 1st April 1961 as one of the schemes of social welfare. Its objectives are: (i) Providing shelter to aged infirm people of the age group 65 and above who have no reasonable source of income and have no one to support. (ii) Providing free food, clothing, beddings and toiletries. (iii) Providing free medical care.

Community based Institutional care

Today all the developed countries have under taken various social, legislative, informative and welfare measures to protect the interests of old people. The United Nations Organisation has declared 1999 as the 'Year of the Older Persons'. Similarly, the Government of India has declared 'National Policy for Older Persons' in 1999 and the year 2000 has been declared as the 'Year of the Older Persons' by our Central Government. 1998-99 the Government of India has declared 'Integrated Programmes for Old Persons.' These programmes include – (i) Day-care Centres, (ii) Mobile Medical Services, (iii) Old-Age-Homes and (iv) Non-Institutional Services. In addition to the above, the Central Government has declared some more remedial measures for old-age problems. These are partial exemption from payment of income-tax, higher rate of interest against savings, traveling facilities and some special facilities for old persons below poverty line (BPL). It is very significant to point out that the Government of India and the State Governments encourage private initiatives also. The Government of India comes with a substantial amount of annual assistance. There are more than 400 old-age homes in India at present. The highest concentration of them is in Pune, Maharashtra. The Help-Age India in Delhi (C-14, Qutab Institutional Area, New Delhi – 110016) is the biggest old age home in India.

In Tripura, it must be highlighted that a few kind-hearted gentlemen have come forward and founded old-aged homes in the vicinity of Agartala. These homes and their founders deserve our respectful attention. The following table speaks about the old-age homes in the state.

It is clear from the above table that all the old-age homes in Tripura are located at West Tripura District. In other three districts of Tripura – Dhalai, South and North Tripura there is no home for old persons. Though Government attempts for alleviation of old-age traumas in our state is far below satisfactory, the state government can claim credit for taking a pioneering step in establishing the first old-age home in Tripura on April 1, 1961. Mention should be made for those respectful, kind-hearted, great gentlemen who came forward and founded old-age homes in the state. Sri Harekrishna Chakraborti, a renowned social activist, took pains to travel widely throughout the state and to popularize old-age homes since last forty years. Mrs. Milan Majumder, Sri. Dilip Pal, Sri. Shyamal Deb, Md. Sirajul Islam, Sri. Jiban Ckakraborti, Sri. Puroshottam Roy Barman

Sl. No.	Name	Year of Estt.	Address	Telephone No.	Remarks
1	2	3	4	5	6
1.	Mahatma Gandhi Old-age Home	01-04-1961	Narsinggarh, Agartala, West Tripura	09436121540	Oldest and the only Govt. Home. For both male/female
2.	Aapnaghar	18-04-1989	Barjala, Airport Road, West Tripura	09863030385	For female only.
3.	Abhoy Ashram	14-11-1991	Sekerkote, Agartala-Bishalgarh Road, West Tripura	0381-2361978	For Hindu Male / Female
4.	Chhayanid	10-12-2002	Indiranagar, Melaghar, West Tripura	09436122515	For Minority Muslim Women.
5.	Sandhyanid	30-04-2004	Dogangi, Gandhigram, West Tripura	0381-2305780/ 0381-2328920	For Both Male / Female
6.	Brajapur Briddhashram		Brajapur, Bishalgarh, West Tripura		Yet to open (Indian Red Cross Society)
7.	Bholananda Matrikashram		Barjala, Near TRTC workshop, West Tripura		Under construction (for female only)
8.	Kathiababa Sebashram		Katlamara, Agartala, West Tripura		Proposed to be constructed.

(Advocate) and Prof. Tapas Dasgupta deserve special mention. Our whole-hearted gratitude is due for those great souls who have been contributing to these old-age homes.

The source of income of these old-age homes in Tripura is multifarious. First of all, a substantial amount is contributed by some generous people of the society. Not only in cash but many magnanimous people donate things (like rice, pulses, vegetables, medicine etc.) in kind. Another good source of income is yearly grants received from the Government of India (Ministry of Social Justice and Empowerment). Sometimes very big old-age homes in India like Help-Age India, Sense International (India), Mobility India and Kolkata Metropolitan Gerontology extend financial assistance to some old-age homes in Tripura. Inmates of some old-age homes like 'Abhoy Ashram' earn something by cottage industry, gardening, poultry, weaving etc. and 60 per cent of this income is compulsorily deposited with the account of the Home. In 2005-06, the amount of financial grant received by some of our old-age homes from the Ministry of Social Justice and Empowerment (Central Govt.) is as follows : (i) Mahatma Gandhi Old-Age Home (Govt.) - @ Rs. 30/- per head is sanctioned by the State Government and the State Government gets financial grant from the Central Government for this purpose; (ii) Aapnaghar : Rs. 4,08,000/-; (iii) Abhoy Ashram : Rs. 2.5 lakhs from the Central Government and Rs. 2.5 lakhs from the Help-Age India; (iv) Chhayanid : Rs. 2,76,412/-; (v) Sanddhyanid : receives no financial help from the Government on principle. The organizers of this home contribute themselves monthly and thus run the home.

Some Proposals

After visiting some old-age homes and talking with the officials and inmates of those homes, I think the attention of the Government and the founders of old-age homes should be drawn on some important points:

i. Rules regarding admission to old-age homes in Tripura are not uniform. This lack of uniformity create scope for foreign nationals (like Bangladeshis) to get shelter in our old-age homes. Here rules framed by the Government of Tripura in 1972 may serve as a model for voluntary agencies also. This code 'Prospectus of Infirmary, 1972' laid down specific rules for admission to old-age homes: (i) Infirm persons of the age 65 and above having Indian Nationality and having no reasonable source of income are eligible for admission. (ii) Above candidates must have a continuous stay of at least 2 years in Tripura state. (iii) Infirm people of the age 65 and above who are suffering only from old-age debility and have no contagious disease are only eligible for admission.

ii. At present the Government of India releases grant-in-aid to old-age homes mainly for food. This is inadequate and insufficient. Grant-in-aid should be sanctioned for other purposes like purchase of land, construction of home, purchase of furniture, utensils etc.

iii. The Union Government sanctions grant-in-aid to old-age homes @ Rs. 12.50/- per day per head. This amount is too poor to meet daily food of an inmate.

Minimum expenditure for the purpose is not less than Rs. 50/- per day today.

iv. The Government of India does not sanction any grant-in-aid to any old age home before receiving Annual Enquiry Report from the State Government. But the principle of 'red tapism', which is inherent in our administration, delays the process. So the Government of Tripura should be more active, punctual, sincere and sympathetic in sending the Annual Enquiry Report of the old-age homes to the Central Government.

v. Expenditure incurred in connection with non-recurring head is met by the central Government after every ten (10) years. Such a gap of time is too long to equip old-age homes timely with necessary and urgent materials. This gap of time requires to be narrowed down shortly.

vi. Another demand of the Silvers' (a term coined now across the world by organizations working for the elderly) in Tripura is ambulance. Aged inmates who are given shelter in homes become sick now and again. So, an ambulance for each home is an immediate need for old-age homes in Tripura.

vii. Our attitude towards silvers should be changed. We should respect them like our parents and close relatives. Inmates of old-age homes should never let feel isolated from the society. We can visit these homes now and then. On the days of national importance like 15th August, 26th and 23rd

January, 14th Nov., 2nd October or 1st Vaisakh we can distribute sweets or clothes to the inmates. Government can encourage the tour of nursery – school children to old-age homes during holidays. NGOs, chemists and druggists or others can distribute medicine to these senior citizens with grey hair. Doctors can render free service to these retired lives.

The Department of Health and Family Welfare, Government of Tripura may come forward with some positive steps. Gerontology, a relatively new science deals with the scientific study of the phenomena of ageing may be opened in two State Hospitals – G.B. and I.G.M. The goal of research in gerontology is to learn more about the ageing process – not for the purpose of extending the life span but so that the disabilities and handicaps of old-age can be minimized. Gerontology utilizes the methodologies of many other scientific disciplines such as biology, genetics, biochemistry, physiology, psychology, medicine and social sciences. So, our University can extend its co-operation in this field.

The Department of Education also has an important role to play. The traditional Indian educational system which would produce non-violent, truthful, honest, pure, continent and respectful citizens is given farewell. Modern education system cannot make a human child a human being; they become unscrupulous and reckless non-human bipeds; they grow into automatons for earning money. So, in our school, college and university syllabi Indian cultural heritage should be given due importance and moral education should be reintroduce for minimizing the problems of aged elders.

In fine, we should embrace age, we need to stop resisting the process and grow old well. The essentials of a silver life are good health and strong bonds, whether they are with family, friends or a vocation. Bertrand Russell (1872-1970), the world famous philosopher, has left for India a significant appeal which may be used for my concluding remark. Russell argues "India is traditionally a land of village communities. It would be a tragedy if this traditional way of life were to be suddenly and violently exchanged for the greater evils of urban industrialism". Gunnar Myrdal also appealed to the Indians in the same tone through his "Asian Drama".

REFERENCES

1. Dr. A. K. Mahapatra, *Bharater Samajik Samasya.*
2. Harekrishna Chakraborti, *Briddhabas ki o keno.*
3. Dr. Pranab Bardhan, *Akhono Sarengeeta Baajchhe.*
4. Sri Harekrishna Chakraborti, a social activist based in Tripura helped me a lot in the preparation of the paper.

9

Magnitude of the Problems of Elderly Persons in Tripura

—Harekrishna Chakraborty

The United Nations organised 1st Global Conference on problems of the older persons at Vienna in Europe in 1982 and designed the Vienna plan of actions for the welfare of the older persons. Again in 2002 the United Nations organized the two global conferences on problem of older persons at Madrid in Europe and reviewed the situation after 1st global conference and designed Madrid plan of action for the welfare of the older persons.

Some other organizations both the international and local NGOs organized such seminars on problems of older persons at different parts of the globe.

United Nations designed International Day of Older Persons, which we observe on 1st October every year.

Moreover, International Association of Gerontology has designed 15th June, 2006 as "World Elder Abuse Awareness Day" with the support of United Nations and World Health Organisation.

Naturally all such big events lead us to think that what has happened to older persons, which make the global society so concerned.

All persons at high age turn gradually weaker and weaker. At the high ageing days they cannot live alone, without others help. Older persons stay with the family. The family referred to is a joint family. Now small nuclear families are being emerged in great numbers and joint family system has been a matter of the past days. Moreover, in these days of globalization citizens roam around the world to get settled with rewarding professions. They abandon their parents and grand parents. And thus older persons become handless at the necessity of high age.

Moreover in the present day circumstances, respect and honour for older persons are at minimum level. Many older persons face abuse, neglect and harassment in our social life. Desire for euthanasia and mercy killing is being developed among older persons.

Older persons are weak entity. So many cases of attacks on their personal life by criminals also take place. In fact security of older persons at present is at high risk.

Some older persons get inflicted with peculiar illness such as Alzheimer's disease (Dementia), Parkinson's disease, Stroke, fall etc. While Arthritis, Cancer, Diabetes & heart Disease are also great problem for the elderly. Morbidity and mortality are more among older persons.

In a sense all these facts have thrown the older persons in trouble.

To keep the older persons lively, many national organizations like Help Age India and local NGOs are now active.

Government of India endorsed National Policy for the older persons and started to implement it, though in low speed. Union Government has some benevolent schemes. Government extends financial assistance to the NGOs for running old age homes and other welfare projects for the elders.

Now let us consider the situation around older persons of Tripura. About 8% of the nearly 30 (thirty) lakhs population of Tripura is in 60+ age group. Their number may be more than 2 (two) lakhs. A big number of them are in below poverty line (BPL). Some BPL holder persons, not all, receive old age pension (National + State).

So far my knowledge is concerned, no survey was organized to asses the plight of elderly persons of Tripura.

In this context, I would like to suggest the following measures (based on personal experience)

1. A Comprehensive survey to be organized to assess the conditions of the older persons in Tripura.
2. Old age pension benefit should be extended to all BPL persons. The pension value should be more than Rs. 500/- (Five hundred) only per month. Present monthly pensions are only Rs. 250/- (Two hundred fifty only) per month. Pension for all elders suggested.
3. Old age homes should be organized for at least

5,000/- (Five thousand) BPL inmates. The present capacity of 5(five) running old age homes in Tripura is not more than 400 (Four hundred).

4. Pay and stay old age homes should be organized to accommodate 1000 (One thousand) older persons. There is a big necessity for such homes. Tripura has no such old age home.
5. A gerontological Research Institute is to be organized. West Bengal has Calcutta Metropolitan Institute of Gerontology.
6. It is very difficult to take care of the bed-ridden in the family. Geriatric care nursing homes are to be organized, one in each District of the State.
7. Dementia patient inflicted with Alzheimer's disease is very difficult to tackle. Alzheimer's victim home is to be organized in the state.
8. Geriatric ward should be opened in all District hospitals of Tripura.
9. Geriatric out patient counter is to be opened in all hospitals of Tripura.
10. Gerontology is to be taught in educational Institutions of Tripura. Elders should be kept in productive ageing program.
11. Anti-ageing life – style is to be popularized among citizens.

Gerontology: The machineries and their functions of the body of older persons are a bit different than those of lower aged normal human beings. The physiology of such declining body health of older persons is termed as gerontology.

Geriatrics: This is medical spatiality of the treatment of ill older persons.

Social Gerontology: This is sociology of gerontological samples i.e. of older persons. This subject studies the distribution of older persons in the society; their living conditions and suggests improvement of their service system.

Ageing: After the middle age body conditions of the human being declines and the person concerned gradually turns weaker and weaker. This phenomenon in general is termed as ageing.

10

Social Security of Old Age Persons in Rural Areas: An Empirical Study

—Jayanta Choudhury

Section-I

Social Security Concepts

The concept of social security had emerged through a long period of evolution. Its history is probably as old as history of men. The quest for survival has prompted mankind, from the beginning of existence, to devise ways of protecting itself from the hazards of life. In primitive societies, the contingencies against which protection was sought centered round the need for self-preservation against the vagaries of nature and external aggression and were largely conditioned by the environment in which people lived. However, with the passage of time, both the nature of contingencies as well as methods developed to meet them, changed a great deal.

Social security, in the modern era is essentially conceived of as a related concept to the high ideals of human dignity and social justice. The working class who plays a major role in the development of the country and contributes directly or indirectly to the country's prosperity should be provided adequate protection against certain risks and hazards to which his/her life is exposed either during the working period or as a consequence thereof. Mostly, these contingencies are economic but in certain cases these hazards may even be social. The concept of social security in a modern welfare state is broad enough to provide comprehensive social security from "Womb to Tomb". The social security system is one of the characteristic institutions mainly developed during the twentieth century. Almost all independent countries have enacted social security measures according to their means and capacity to pay. The modern industrial society and the system of the present century have unequivocally recognized the importance of covering workers from various risks, especially when the old social structure is fast disintegrating owing to the rapid growth of industrialized life.

The concept of social security has various dimensions. After the emergence of the Industrial Revolution, the governments of various countries have been forced to adopt policies and programmes of social security within their respective constitutional set up. Today almost all the democratic and socialist countries of the world have their own pattern of social security structure for a regulated social order.

Social security is a worldwide phenomenon which has acquired global attention in recent years. Social Security seeks to provide financial assistance to the rural needy people apart from the legal protection which has been provided to industrial or organized labourers. But unfortunately no uniform or standard definition has been given the word 'social security'. The reason of such irony could be variation in the nature of social security from country to country. In this regard the International Labour Organization (ILO) has put it effort to define the term social security as " the protection – furnished by society to its members through a series of public measures against the economic and social distress that otherwise would be caused by the absences of earnings or substantial reduction or stoppage of earnings resulting from sickness, maternity, employment injury (including occupational diseases), unemployment (including absences of employment) and underemployment, invalidity, destitution, social disability and backwardness, old age and death, and further, to provide for health care, including preventive measures".

The concept of social security is based on ideals of human dignity and socio-economic justice. Underlying the concept is also the desire to give protection to its citizens who contribute to a country's total welfare, against certain hazards to which they are exposed either in the working life or as a consequence of it. These hazards are essentially economic though in some cases they may even be social. Social security, in other words, insures a person against economic distress resulting from various contingencies and ensures him a minimum level of living consistent with the nation's capacity to pay.

According to *Lexicon Universal Encyclopedia*, the term 'Social security' is defined as "Social security consists of public programmes intended to protect workers and their families from income loses associated with old age, illness, unemployment or death. The term is sometimes also used to include a broad system of support for all those, who for whatever reasons are unable to maintain themselves".

The above definitions can be conveniently analyzed into following components:

Schemes endorsed and regulated by the government or some public authority on its behalf for the purpose of protecting workers and their families are designated as social security programme;

Under these schemes financial protection is provided to the workers or their independent cases of loses of employment, injury, old age invalidity or death, and

Schemes of providing financial assistance to the persons unable to meet their necessities irrespective of any reason are also included within the term social security.

W A Robson defines social security somewhat comprehensively as follows: "Social security is a way of ensuring freedom from want or poverty which is one of the formidable obstacles in the way of progress. Social security implies insurance against those misfortunes to which an individual remains exposed even when the condition of society as a whole improves. It does not include the various measures for improving the conditions of society-full employment, minimum wage, factory law, public health, housing, education and so forth".

The peculiarity of the above definition is that it lays stress on individual welfare guaranteed by general social progress. The definition also specifically excludes certain items from the term of social security. The main emphasis in the definition is to show that social progress and individual happiness are not identical. The individual continue to face troubles and misfortunes even when society as a whole improves. Often this causes the imbalance and misdistribution of the benefits of social progress.

The National Commission on Labour defined the concept of Social Security as "The term Social security envisages that the members of the community shall be protected by collective action against social risks causing undue hardship and privation to individual whose private resources can seldom be adequate to meet them. The concept of social security is based on ideals of human dignity and social justice. The underlying idea behind social security measures is that a citizen who has contributed or is likely to contribute to his country's welfare should be given protection against certain hazards".

All the above definitions stress one or other aspects of social security. These aspects include income maintenance, medical care and covering of contingencies and risks. The latest trend in the definition seems to require provisions of preservation of acquired standard of living and ensuring social minimum to those individual in the society who are exposed to various inevitable social and economic risks despite general prosperity and who by their own means cannot provide for the same. The benefits generally covered by social security schemes, as reflected or inferred from various aforesaid definitions are medical care, sickness benefit, unemployment benefit, old age benefit, maternity benefit, invalidity benefit, survivor's benefit and so on. All definitions speak of the ever-increasing role of the state in general and the role of employers and the labour in particular. The degrees of the shares of each depend on merits of each case and on the expediency of the situation.

In brief, the meaning of social security can be categorized in two ways such as (i) legal protection and (ii) social assistance. In the frame of legal protection it covers all basic facilities, compensation, working conditions etc for all those workers who engaged in industrials units or works in joint form. Whereas in case of financial assistance it covers needy sections of the society who are unable to get day-to-day's necessities due to poverty, sickness, old age, grief atmosphere of the family etc.

Section-II

Social Security Schemes

The agencies which have been spearheading the movement for social security consist of both voluntary and governmental agencies. However, the voluntary agencies, which sometimes run on the basis of religion or community, strictly confine their activities within perimeter of group interests. Looking at the prevalence of various structures of social security schemes, we can conveniently group the same in the following basic categories:

Non-statutory social security schemes, and

Statutory social security schemes.

i) Non-statutory social security schemes

Earlier, non-statutory schemes were only measures available to save the depressed classes from the social evils of poverty and misfortunes. These schemes were introduced without any aid from the government and were organized by people of a certain community or by people of certain profession. They were mainly divided into three types:

Schemes run by voluntary organizations,

Public assistance, and

Gratuitous benefits provided by the employers to the workers.

a) *Schemes run by voluntary organizations*

The voluntary organization which were motivated by the idea of providing benefits only to the members of their own folks i.e. on the basis of community or caste, received regular or intermittent funds from the members of their particular community or caste. Thus, the friendly societies of Great Britain, being voluntary organizations, covered within its activity the old people, the workers, and persons from other important profession. These organizations provided insurance against illness and other similar contingencies, which resulted in loss of income to the workers. However similar organizations were subsequently formed in the United States and in many other countries of the world. At that time, trade organizations took a pioneering part in arranging for help against sickness, accidents or unemployment due to strike or lockout. Such organizations were, however, very unorganized and had no definite period of existence and in most cases they were dissolved after some time. Another drawback of these organizations was that persons of only selected financial back ground could join such organizations. Distress funds opened in the voluntary organization or any particular organization may be mentioned as an instance of this kind.

b) *Public assistance*

The schemes for providing public assistance in the form of family allowances, unemployment allowance, old age pension allowances, to the needy and the helpless persons was initially introduced in the advanced countries which were committed to the principles of public welfare. Public consciousness in these countries is indeed one of the causes for such transformation of ideas on the part of government, leading to provision of such basic amenities. These benefits were first provided in countries like France, United States, Britain, Canada etc., followed by Denmark and Sweden.

However, with the passing of diverse legislations in the field of social security, many such benefits are automatically available for his/her being a worker. It is against this backdrop of growing tendency for legislation in the arena of social security, that the public assistance programmes lost its significance. However, in the third world countries where the problem of unemployment have assumed menacing proportions, public assistance is emerging as a strong weapon to deal with wide spread social tensions particularly caused by the frustration among youths. The poverty situation also cannot give rise to the formation of so many voluntary organizations, which could take care of the old infirm and physically and mentally handicapped. In India a number of State

Governments have already announced schemes for payment of unemployment allowances, old age pension and concessional transport service to the old and ailing citizens. The alarming unemployment situation in India has forced its government to seriously consider introduction of right to work as a fundamental right in the Indian Constitution. However, such public assistance programmers have also suffered from paucity of funds in the past and their continuity is subject to availability of funds from the government kitty.

c) *Gratuitous benefits provided by the employers to the workers*

Prior to the passing of the social security legislation in most countries of the world, a system prevailed under which the employer paid compensation to the employee in the case of his injury or engaged him in alternative job just to provide him with continuity of service. Although this was essential to preserve the high morale of employees, yet its voluntary nature could not ensure or guarantee any sort of uniformity and dependability in the wishes employers. As such, these considerations as were made by certain employers purely developed upon their human considerations and ability to afford payment, since the entire payment was the burden upon the individual employer or his group.

ii) Statutory schemes

The well being of the people, which is the major common concern for any government committed to the ideal of welfare state, has been conceived of by almost all countries of the world as the first essential step for steady and rapid economic growth. This led to the passing of various Acts some of which had their basis on the occupational distribution of workers while others had general applicability in respective fields. However, the quantum of benefits, qualifying period, nature and extent of risk covered under the statutory schemes vary from country to country and within the same country too they vary at two different times. This statutory nature of aid mainly takes two forms viz., social assistance and social insurance. The system of social security made it appearance in India at a later stage than in many of industrially developed countries mainly for her slow growth in industrialization.

At present, social security legislations in India comprises the Workermen's Compensation Act 1923; the Central and State Maternity Acts; the Employee's State Insurance Act 1948, the Coal Mines Provident Fund and Bonus Schemes Act 1948; the Employee Provident Fund and Pension Fund Act 1952; Industrial Employment Standing Orders act 1946, Gratuity Act 1972, etc cover risk, create working atmosphere and provide monetary benefit to the employees.

In present situation social security is a socio-economic demand of every society irrespective of its political creed. It seeks to compensate for underserved wants, disabilities, inequalities and deprivation of the established socio-economic order. It offers the underprivileged the dignity, self-confidence, belief in just society and new means for moral, social and material betterment. Its importance is now-a-days universal owing to urge for balanced economic growth, awakening of rights of the individual in the society, emergence of welfare state and other factors.

The Constitution of India contains provisions relating to various aspects of the welfare of people. The various article in Part IV of the Indian Constitution, which have direct or indirect bearing on social security measures and legislation are Articles 38(2), 39(e) and (f),41, 43,47.

Article 38(2): "The state shall, in particular strive to minimize the inequalities in income and endeavour to eliminate inequalities of States and opportunities, not only among individuals but also among of people residing in different areas or engaged in different vocation".

Article 39(e): "The state shall in particular direct its policy towards securing than the health and strength of workers, men and women, and the tender age of children are not abused and that citizen are not forced by economic necessity to enter avocations unsuited to their age and strength".

Article 39(f): "The state shall, in particular direct its policy towards securing that children are given opportunities and facilities to develop in a healthy manner and in conditions of freedom and dignity and that childhood and youth are protected against exploitation and against moral and maternal abandonment".

Article 41: "The state shall within the limits of its economic activity and development, make effective provisions for securing the right to work, to education and to public assistance in cases of unemployment, old age, sickness and disablement and in other cases of undeserved want"

Article 42: "The state shall make provision for securing just and human conditions of work and for their maternity relief."

Article 43: "Provides that states shall strive to secure living wage, a decent standard of life and full employment of leisure and social and culture opportunities to all the workers, agriculture and industrial or otherwise" and

Article 47: "Impose a duty on the state to raise the level of nutrition and the standard of living and to improve public health".

These Articles reproduced above are intended to secure, besides social security measures, a new social order in which the citizens are assured of socio-economic justice. Among these Art.41, directly relates to the social security of the elderly population. To implement the ideas in the Directive Principle of State Policy both the central as well as state governments are empowered to enact legislation in relation to 'labour' as embodied in list III (The concurrent list) of Seventh Schedule of Indian Constitution. Entry 23 of this list deals with "social security and insurance", employment and un-employment. Again entry 24 of this list deals with 'welfare of labour' including conditions of work, provident funds, employer's liability, workmen's compensation, invalidity, old age pension and maternity benefits. Consequently various social security legislation like employee's state insurance Act, 1948, employees' provident fund Act, 1952, Maternity Benefit Act, 1961 and Gratuity Act, 1972, were enacted which are widely known as instrumentalities of social security system in India.

After independence, almost all states and union territories have implemented their own rules in favour of providing financial assistance to disabled, destitute widows and aged persons. As far as implementation of social security programme for rural poor is concerned, Uttar Pradesh is the first State in India which introduced social security programme in 1957 which later on was followed by other States/Union territories between 1960 and 1970s. Some of the States have introduced social security programme in different years such as Government of Rajasthan (1967), Government of Madhya Pradesh (1970), Government of Punjab (1968), Government of Karnataka (1965), Government of Maharashtra (1980), Government of Kerala (1960), and Government of Tamil Nadu (1962) for the welfare of above-mentioned people. The pensions of these groups are revised from time to time. In case of many States and Union Territories the states Old Age Pension is clubbed with the National Old Age pension. Many State Governments do have a provision of distribution of free cloth, food-grain, mid-day meals, nutrition intake to the pregnant women etc as additional benefit to the beneficiaries.

Section –III

Social Security of Elderly Persons in Tripura

Ageing is now recognized as a global major social, economic and humanitarian issue. The *Oxford Dictionary* defines old age as the later part of the normal age. There are two main approaches to the identification and definition of old age which are biological and chronological. Biologically, normal ageing is characterized by progressive and irreversible change in both structure and function of the body with time. In modern society we use chronological age i.e the length of the time that a person lived as an indicator of age.

National Old Age Pension Scheme (NOAPS)

National Social Assistance Programme (NSAP), which came into effect from 15th August 1995, represents a significant step towards the fulfillment of Directive Principles in Articles 41 and 42 of the Constitution through the enunciation of a National policy for social assistance benefits to the poor households in the case of old age, death of breadwinner and maternity. National Old Age Pension Scheme (NOAPS) is one of the three components of NSAP. The aims of the programme are to provide financial assistance to the aged people for a better life, some pleasant and happiness, their required respects and sympathy. This is given to the destitute. The amount is a meager Rs. 125 per month (revised to Rs.300 subsequently).

Under this scheme central assistance is available as per following criteria:

1. The age of the applicant (male/female) is sixty five years or more.
2. The applicant is a destitute in the sense having little or no regular means of subsistence from his or her own sources of income or through financial support from family or other sources.

Objectives of the Study

To asses the efficiency of the programmes in terms of coverage, potentialities and effectiveness.

To measure the progress in both quantitative as well

as qualitative aspects in relation to the stated objectives targets.

To identify the major loopholes of the programme and suggest recommendation for betterment of the programmes to achieve its desired goals.

Study Methodology

As the programme is implemented universally to all villages through out the state, for the present study, one village was selected randomly. The study was conducted at the Lankamura village West District of Tripura. Secondary data was collected from concerned Panchayat office and Block office and primary data was collected from the village by household survey through well structured schedule. All the beneficiaries under NOAPS i.e. 71 beneficiaries were covered. An efficiency Index was prepared for assessing the performance of the programme.

No. of really benefited people under the programme × 100
Goal Efficiency Index (GE I) = Total no. of beneficiaries.
Actual eligible candidates × 100
Potentiality Efficiency Index (PEI) =Actual candidates + No. of potential candidates
No. of present beneficiaries
CEI = × 100Capacity of program
Evaluation Index (EI) = (GEI +PEI +CEI) × 1/3

Major Findings:

Out of total beneficiaries, 36.7 per cent were male and 63.3 were female. Total 77.3 per cent were from Schedule Caste categories. All of them were from BPL family. Total 23.3 per cent beneficiaries were receiving assistance for less than 3 years, 33.3 per cent were receiving assistance for 4-5 years and rest 43.4 per cent were assisted for more than 5 years old.

The three Efficiency Index for NOAPS programme.

GEI = (71 / 71) X 100 = 100per cent
PEI = 50/ (71+50) X 100 = 41.32per cent
CEI = (71/71) X 100 = 100per cent
EI = (100+41.32+100) / 3 = 80.44per cent

The above three efficiency index evaluate the performance of the programme.

As the GEI is found to be 100 per cent, it can be inferred that the programme has fully achieved its specific goals.

The PEI of this programme clearly indicates the failure of the programme with regard to the selection of the beneficiaries. This index is rather low (41.32per cent), compared to other index.

The performances of the CEI is also indicates it has fulfilled its capacity. So the Evaluation Index which is the mean of above three indices, indicate that the performance of NOAPS has been satisfactory.

Major loopholes

- Lack of awareness about the scheme among the villagers
- The amount of assistance is very less.
- Disbursement after every three months.
- The number of beneficiaries is not adequate.

- Selection of the beneficiaries is not transparent.
- Delay in sanction.
- Poor monitoring system.

Policies for Better Performances:

1. For the selection of actual beneficiaries following steps should be taken

- Wide publicity is necessary through all levels of administration mainly at Panchayat, with the help of awareness camp, canvassing and with other mass communicators mainly radio, posters etc.
- The block level authority should strictly assess the economic condition of the candidates regarding the selection of beneficiary and it should be done honestly.

2. Proper monitoring and evaluating machinery for this programme should be devised. Government may appoint young professional in each District Level. Their services may also be used for effective implementation of other programmes.
3. States also should responsible for successful implementation of this NOAPS programme.

State Government Union Territory and Government of India should create medical facilities and income generation programme as much as possible for the aged population.

Role of NGOs and VOs

Government should work collaboratively with NGOs and VOs. They play very good role for any successful programme, which are pointed out below in short.

a) They make wide publicity and awareness through their own style and machinery.

b) They are helpful in monitoring and evaluating of the programme.

c) There are three basic necessities for the elderly today–financial security, health security and emotional security. Several NGOs performed effectively for reducing this problem.

A) Financial security: There are 30 NGOs working in this regard at local level. At National level, big NGO like Help Age India provides these facilities through animal husbandry and life-stock, vegetation, for processing, candle and envelop making etc. which require very little physical labour.

B) Health security: A lot of NGOs at the rural level are involved in community based heath care through mobile medicare units (MMU). NGOs help restoration of vision by getting cataract surgeries performed for financially weak elderly in various village in India.

C) Emotional security: NGOs like Day care centre(all over country) give the elderly a chance to share their joys and sorrows with persons of their own age group as well as earn some money from income generation projects during their stay there, from morning till evening.

Conclusion

Government is trying heart and soul for the aged persons. Several other programme and schemes has been launched in different plan period. The sufferings of aged persons have become a matter of concern for everyone.

NGOs/VOs are working jointly to reduce the problem of old-age people. Today the aged persons are related as parasites of the family. They are not getting their minimum required respect and sympathy. So they are feeling themselves cursed. But younger generation should think that they also have to pass in that pathetic situation in the old age. So they should obey their early generation and utilize their experience to eradicate their daily-life problems.

REFERENCES

1. Chandra, Suman(1996): "Course on Social security for the poor in Unorganised Sector". *Reading Material.* National Institute of Rural Development, Hyderabad.

2. Government of Kerala (1995): *National Social Assistance Programme* 'GO (P) No.47/95 Social Welfare Department, Thiruvanathapuram.

3. Government of Rajasthan (1995): "*National Social Assistance Programme*" Rural Development and Panchayati Raj, Jaipur.

4. Ministry of Rural development, Government of India (1995), *Guideline of National Social Assistance Programme,* New Delhi.

5. Nair, Sobha B (1990) *Social Security and the Weaker Section* Renaissance Publishing House, Delhi.

6. Najmul Hasan 'Social Security Planning in India' *Yojana,* vol 17, No 14, 1973, pp 587-590.

7. Note on "National Social Assistance Programmein India".

8. Sikligar, P C (2000): *Social security* Mangal Deep Publications, Jaipur.

11

The Socio-Economic Status of the Elderly People: A Case Study of Malabati Tea Estate in Tripura

—Partha Sengupta

Sources of Data and Methodology

SURVEY SPOT: Malabati Tea Estate

LOCATION: Sekerkote, Bisalgarh Sub-Division, West Tripura

PERIOD OF SURVEY: Three Days from 28 Nov 2006 to 30 Nov 2006

NO, OF FAMILY VISITED: 25 (Twenty five)

NUMBER OF ELDERLY PEOPLE CONSULTED: 8 (Eight)

NO. OF CASES MENTIONED IN THE PAPER: 5

METHOD APPLIED: Sample Survey Method

NO. OF FAMILIES HAVING ELDERLY PEOPLE: 10

PEOPLE CONSIDERED AS ELDERLY: Those who have attained 65 years

Points of Enquiry

1. AGE OF RETIREMENT
2. FINANCIAL SUPPORT
3. DISEASES THEY SUFFER FROM
4. FOOD HABIT AND FOOD PROVISIONS
5. OLD AGE PENSION
6. WHETHER SEXUAL DISCRIMINATION EXISTS
7. ATTITUDE OF FAMILY MEMBERS TO ELDERLY FAMILY MEMBERS
8. SOCIAL ACCEPTANCE
9. MODE OF PASSING TIME

General Observation

Like many other tea estate of Tripura, Malabati Tea Estate is no exception relating in terms of natural beauty. It is just 12km away from Battala, Agartala. It is a small tea garden, naturally the number of workers family is not big. At present the number of daily rated worker working in this tea estate is only 45. As I have noticed the socio-economic position of the elderly people is miserable. Workers are sent to retirement at the age of 65. While in working state a worker is paid in cash just Rs.30.00 per day on the basis of presence. Gratuity scheme has not been introduced. Pension scheme is a day dream to the elderly people of Malabati Tea Estate. Therefore, superannuation leads to an uncertainty that the elderly people of the tea estate have to face.

Actual Cases

Case I

Malati Tanti– An elderly widow of 72 years.

In course of conversation, she told that her forefather was a resident of Bihar. She is now an elderly widow of 72 years. She has a BPL (Below Poverty Line) card. Once she was a worker of the tea estate. She has got no pension facility from the garden scheme after retirement. However, Rs 125/- is provided by the Bikramnagar Panchayat as old age pension. She has two sons. One of them is dead. She is now under the care of her only living son earning Rs 30 as a worker of the garden and this is the only source of regular income. The family is in the grip of intense poverty. Her husband died in 1986. She is suffering from high level blood pressure, disorder of stomach and some other water borne diseases. Physically she looks very lean and thin. She lives with her son and daughter-in-law having two children. She is found to be well bonded. Everybody around her respects her. She passes her time by making chitchat with her neighbours.

Case II

Durga Gowala: An elderly widower of 74years.

Durga Gowala's forefather hailed from Vilashpur, Bihar. He is 74years old and retired from daily labour work. He gets old age pension Rs. 125/- per month from Bikramnagar Panchayat. No other regular source of income is there for him. He is the father of three sons and two daughters. His wife is dead. Mainly his elder son takes care of him. He has married off his daughters. He suffers from chest pain, respiratory problems and high blood pressure. There are two grand children on his lap. He is pleased with his present state of family. He passes time doing some light work and gossiping with his neighbours. He wants to live more just to see his grandsons growing up.

Case III

Gandhya Raj Tanti: An infirm old man of 82 years

Once he used to work as a daily labourer outside the garden, later he worked in the garden for a few days. But being physical by unfit became jobless at the age of 62. Since then he has been living a life full of diseases like high blood pressure, respiratory problems. He is not getting requisite medicine being infirm to move about he was found lying in bed. Financial support is very weak. Rs 125/- is given as old age pension by the Panchayat. His wife works as a daily labourer and earns Rs.30 per day to meet the daily expenses of five members. A small thatched bamboo hut accommodates all the five members and the same room is used as a kitchen. A bleak picture unfolded as rice is found boiling and a paste of wild leaves is prepared to be eaten with rice. Two grandchildren are there. They belong to his daughter living with him. He wants to live more just to see his grandson grow up well fit do his job.

Case IV

Simo Tanti: Unafraid of death at 72 years

She gets no allowance. She has two daughters and five sons. She often suffers from stomach pain and chest pain. Daughters are married. Only two sons live with her who work in the garden as daily labourers. Other sons work at Kutrabai, Bangladesh. But they do not send any sort of financial aid to her. She is found very firm about onset of death. She told me that one morning one of her grandchildren would call her while she would be in sleeping state and he or she would not get any response and thought that she. She passes time by way of chatting with neighbour and taking due care of her grandchildren. Now and then she takes part in collecting firewood from jungle. The hut she lives in is made of mud and bamboo. Financially she lives a life below poverty line but she is not holding BPL card. Inspite of having different types of diseases she can't avail medical care. She told that winter is a curse in her life because she has no warm clothes to prevent the ravages of winter. In response to my question as to how sensitive her family members feel to her sufferings, she was found thinking deeply. After a while she responded in a low voice that her sons are to a certain extent sensitive to feel the sufferings of her pain at this age and that's why they try their level best to hear and to meet her demands. She also says that she can realize their limitations. She was found very much worried about the forthcoming winter as it would bring nothing but intense sufferings for a woman like her. She is found socially well accepted. People of her age appreciated her dealings with them. In the family she is found well accomodated on a bamboo made cot. Her grandchildren were found playing in the dusty yard infront of her hut. Attitude of other members to her is considerably healthy, that's why she wants to live more.

Case V

Laxmi Tanti: A young old worker of 64 years

Laxmi Tanti works in the tea garden as a daily rated

labourer at a payment of Rs.30/- paid on the basis of her presence in the work site. At this age she has to work just to keep her family alive. Her husband died years ago and her only earning son is physically unfit after a truck accident at Dharmangar, North Tripura. Since then she has been shouldering the burden of a family consisting of eight members–four grandchildren, one unmarried daughter of 16 years and a son along with her daughter-in-law, who was found entering carrying a pitcher. When I asked whether she also earns for the family she nodded negatively. Smt Laxmi Tanti is not holding BPL card. I could not make out how a family having eight members can survive with an earning of Rs.30 a day. She is found in fragile health condition and is suffering from severe headache along with joint pain and respiratory problems. Being the only earning member she is treated well in the family. The daughter-in-law was found expressing deep concern about her and told what would be if her mother-in-law falls ill. Laxmi Tanti was also worried about the future of her daughter who has dropped out of school on account of financial insecurity. In spite of intense poverty, Smt Laxmi Tanti is found expressing a sense of acceptance of her fate. She told me that she is getting due respect from the family as well as from the society she lives in. She told that she is not worried about death rather she is worried about the fate of the family in her absence.

All other cases revealed almost same facts. My investigation leads me to conclude that the elderly people of those families do get due honour but suffer a fate of destitute life in different aspects because of weak financial status.

Appendix

State Policy on Older Persons

Introduction

Extension of health care facilities, economic development and State sponsored welfare activities and spread of education, though unevenly, since the first five year plan have considerable improved life expectancy among people in India leading to increase in the number of persons 60+. From only 20 million of such persons in 1951, the number crossed 57 million in 1991 in India and in percentage terms, persons 60+ in the total population has a steady rise from 5.1% in 1901 to 6.8% in 1991. It is expected to reach 8.9% in 2016. Tripura is not exception to the national phenomenon in terms of percentage of senior citizens.

Family ties in India are still very strong and the majority of persons 60+ live with their children supported by them. Moreover, working couples find the presence of old parents emotionally bonding and of great help in managing house-hold and caring for children. In many cases, emerging socio-economic problem coupled with changed out-look stand in the way of persons of 60+ being looked after by their children. Much higher cost of bringing up and educating children, shortage of space in dwellings in urban areas, adoption of small family norms, employment out-side have also reduced care giving to the old person by their children.

The problem of care giving is much more serious among lower income group and people living below poverty line. Children of these categories are not in a position to extend care and higher costs to meet health and other needs of their persons on account of harsh economic realities and penuary. Widows and females are more vulnerable in old age because an overwhelming majority of whom have no independent source of income, don not own assets and are totally dependent. Tripura is a tiny state full of hills and hillocks with a population of 27,57,205 as per 1991 census. Out of the total population, 30.95% belongs to Scheduled Tribe and 16.35% to the Scheduled Caste Community. Backwardness is rampant in all sectors of the economy such as trade, business, commerce, industry and agriculture. As a result 74% of the population live below poverty line and the per capita income is much below the national average. The magnitude of the problem is giving care to senior citizens which will therefore, be higher in Tripura than in other relatively developed states of the country. So demographic, socio-economic and epidemiological issues caused by increasing elderly population of Tripura call for urgent measures to cope with them. If the State does not plan out measures right now to face the issues, the present generation of youths may have to spend their old age in misery and deprivation.

Policy Objectives

i. The State Policy espouses the concerns of older persons as state concerns and will see that they are not-treated as liability and spent-up-force, but as a productive and participating population group.

ii. The policy recognizes the strengthening of State's age-long family tradition of giving care to the elderly by families as the first and major step in the care of the aged.

iii. The policy envisages that the State with the assistance of the Central Government would extend support for financial security, health care, shelter, welfare and other needs of older persons.

iv. The policy seeks to make available opportunities for development of the potential of Older persons and seek their participation in nation building work so they themselves feel worthy and live the last phase of their live with dignity and purpose.

v. The policy believes the older persons as productive assets. They render useful services in the family and outside. It will encourage the arrangement of privileges to the elderly in different service-counters to case their service rendering.

vi. The policy seeks to give special care to the vulnerable groups among the elderly widows, disabled, infirmed and destitute.

vii. The policy realizes that the state can not alone attain the objectives. Individuals, families, communities have to join hand as partners in attaining the cherished objectives. NGOs are to play a very crucial role in implementation of programmes meant for the welfare of the elderly. Involvement of NGOs could be encouraged.

Action Strategies Financial Security

i. In a backward State like Tripura where 74% of the people live below poverty line, financial insecurity is felt most acutely. The existing old age pension scheme meant for persons 60+ need to be extended to cover all elders living below poverty line. Attempt will also be made to cover the old persons of lower income group (above poverty line) to instill in them a sense of security.

ii. Prevention of delays in the disbursement of monthly pension under the existing scheme and the periodical revision of the amount of pension on the basis of price rise are necessary for attaining its purpose meaningfully.

iii. Pension is a much sought after income security scheme for seeking out livelihood in old age. A large number of self-employed and salaried non-Government employees are not covered under any sort of old age security measure. Motivational-cum-counseling programmes will be encouraged to take root in Tripura the need for saving, under the existing pensionary schemes run by public sector financial institutions, a portion of their income during the active working years, for financial security in old age.

iv. It will be considered if a comprehensive enactment can be made conferring rights of parents without means to be supported by their children.

Health Care and Nutrition

i. In advancing stage, older persons generally suffer from myriad health problems requiring long term treatment of illness, constant attention as it involves the risk of disability, Health-care facilities free of cost are easily accessible to all categories of population of the State including the elderly in the Government run Hospitals, PHC and Dispensaries and the facilities are more or less adequate. What is to be done now is to ensure that the elderly patients are not subjected to long waits and visits to different counters for medical test and treatment. Health Department will endeavour to provide separate counters and convenient timings on specified days.

ii. Old-age diseases are mostly different from common diseases and require expertise treatment and test. A mobile geriatic unit also needs to be attached to the District Hospitals to conduct medical check-up and, to provide medicines to the vulnerable elderly like old, kinless widows, disabled and chronically ill at modified points in the District concerned.

iii. It will be endeavored to give orientation programme on the health and nutrition of the elderly and the ways to meet them to elder persons and their families through brochures, leaflets and mass media as health care measure.

Welfare

i. Efforts will be made to set up old-age Home at District / Sub-Divisional level especially for the poor, the kin-less and the abandoned through the NGOs under Central / State Schemes. Qualified professional staff to assure minimum standard of quality service with the aim of ensuring minimum well-being of inmates of these Homes would be developed.

ii. NGOs are also to be assisted and encouraged for setting up Old-age Homes for middle and lower middle class/group of families. NGOs may charge reasonable monthly payment for each client of this group in exchange for the care and services to be rendered.

iii. Older persons will be encouraged to form informal groups of their own in the neighbourhood which will satisfy the needs for social interaction, and other activities. For a group of neighborhood/ villages, the formation of senior citizens forum will be encouraged.

iv. It will be endeavoured to arrange priority que use for the elderly in all booking and service counters in places like transport offices, hospitals, gas-cylinder department telephone bill counter, bank, post office, etc.

v. Gaon panchayat will be encouraged and assisted to keep and maintain a register of persons 60+ particularly those who are below poverty line. The Gaon Panchayats will be the contact group for all programmes meant for the elderly.

vi. All communication channels will be used to inculcate the values of love and respect for the elders and show adequate care for them.

vii. Individuals of all ages, families and communities will be provided information about ageing process and changing role-responsibilities and relationship at different stage of life cycle. The contribution of elder persons inside house-hold and outside will be highlighted through the media and other forums as a measure of strengthening family bond and tradition.

Research

Research activity on ageing is considered to be very important aspect as far as the welfare activities of the elderly are concerned. Academic bodies like University and Research Institutions will be encouraged and assisted to go into the problems of older persons, evaluate ongoing programmes and identify new and potential areas in the perspective of Tripura.

Gerontologists will also be assisted to strengthen research findings and provide a platform for dialogue, discussions, debate and exchange of information.

Implementation/Administration

i. An action plan to give effect to the policy will be prepared so that its feature remains in constant public focus.

ii. The Department of Social Welfare and Social Education will be the nodal department to coordinate all matters relating to the implementation of the Policy. A separate cell for Older persons will be set-up in the department to exclusively deal with the issues. An inter departmental committee with Minister/ Secretaries of the relevant departments will be set up to coordinate matters relating to implementation of the State Policy and to monitor its progress.

iii. The State Planning Department and Finance

Department will facilitate budgetary provisions required for implementation of the Policy. The State Planning Board will recognize ageing as a priority area and incorporate ageing as a special component in all areas of planning.

iv. Every three years, the nodal department on the implementation of the policy will do a detailed review. There will be non-official participation in the review work.

v. The immense potentiality of NGOs will be accepted and they would be actively involved in the promotion and implementation of the Policy.

vi. Panchayat Raj Institutions will be encouraged to participate in the implementation of the Policy and address local level issues and needs of the ageing and implement programmes for them. Social Justice Committees of village Panchayats in particular are to advocate different measures for giving effect to the policy.

* * Published in Tripura Gazette, dated 28th November, 2000

Index

■■■